People once believed that when a person died,

a crow carried their soul to the land of the dead.

But sometimes, something so bad happens that a terrible

sadness is carried with it; and the soul can't rest.

Then sometimes, just sometimes, the crow can bring that soul back

to make the wrong things right.

WRITER · JEFF CONNER
PHOTOGRAPHER · ROBERT ZUCKERMAN

Much thanks and praise to Edward R. Pressman, James O'Barr, Jeff Most, Robert Zuckerman
and John Bergin for advice and support, as well as all of the participants who put up with me
during this project (especially Tamara, Michael, Jamie and Denis at Kitchen Sink Press).

—Jeff Conner

There are many people to whom I am grateful for their support, encouragement and inspiration.

To David Mamet, for recommending me to Ed Pressman.

To Ed Pressman, Neil Friedman, Pamela Godfrey, Michael Radiloff, Daniel Posener,
Emily Zalenski and other members of Pressman Films for making it happen and staying with it.

To Alex Proyas, Bob Rosen and the crew of THE CROW for their commitment, faith and vision.

To Dariusz Wolski, Claudio Miranda, Steve Andrews and Chunky Huse for light and access.

To Jeff Conner, Jeff Most, David Schow, Greg Gale, Harry Clein, Kimberly Glann, Jason Scott and
Cara White; to Denis Kitchen, Tamara Sibert and Kevin Russell of Kitchen Sink Press; to Andy,
Danielle, Andrea and others at Studio Photo Service in Hollywood, and Brenda at G.P. Color for
their diligence, energy and care in bringing this book to fruition.

To the loved ones, family and friends of Brandon Lee.

To my family, Margot, Evelyn, Ruth, Matthew, Leslie, Patricia and Paul; my friends, Bianca Rossini,
Joel Levinson, Andrei, Gigi and Liz Ridgeway; to the memory of Charlie, Isobel, Helen, Morris,
Jim, Gerald, Eric, Carol, Stuart, Guy, Chino and others who illuminate the eternal road.

To James O'Barr for his quiet, steadfast spirit.

To Brandon, for the fire that burns inside.

—Robert Zuckerman

EDITORS · PHILIP AMARA & MICHAEL EASTMAN
ART DIRECTOR · TAMARA SIBERT
DESIGNERS · MICHAEL EASTMAN & TAMARA SIBERT
ADDITIONAL ASSISTANCE · CHRIS COUCH,
KEVIN LISON, BRENDAN STEPHENS AND LISA STONE

THE CROW: THE MOVIE © 1994 Crowvision. ISBN 1 85286 652 7
Published by Titan Books Ltd, 42-44 Dolben Street, London SE1 0UP
First British edition May 1995.

4 6 8 10 9 7 5 3

PRINTED IN CANADA

THE CROW

THE MOVIE

Jeff Conner & Robert Zuckerman

FOR BRANDON

I have stretched ropes from steeple to steeple;

garlands from window to window;

golden chains from star to star,

and I dance.

—Rimbaud

THE CROW
THE MOVIE

Brandon

And he has left us.
yet, in his absence,
His presence is
And shall be
Stronger than ever.

For he is
everywhere now,
And he is
inside of us;

We, who witnessed
The brilliance
Of his flame
And were warmed
by its heat;

We, who heard
the chimes
of his churchbell laughter
Ring the plains
of starry dawns;

We, who stood
in the pure rain
of his divine
And noble spirit
Are now its
blessed, honored keepers.

Within and through us
He shall live on
And our lives
Shall ever be enriched
By him
in ways
Wondrous and untold.

Fly high, dear friend.

—Robert Zuckerman
March 31, 1993

THE CROW was completed to honor Brandon Lee.

There was a time when it seemed the film would never see the light of day. All of us who had worked with him were devastated by the loss of Brandon; finishing the film was the farthest thing from anyone's mind.

But people started to rally behind completing it. First several members of the cast, then Brandon's friends and family, expressed their feeling that Brandon would want his work to be seen.

I think they were right.

Brandon had put his heart into his character—he really cared about this film and wanted it to be something special. I think that shows.

There will always be a lot of justifiable anger over Brandon's death, but there is one glimmer of optimism here—the film itself—Brandon's film. In years to come people will still be as dazzled by his brilliance as we were.

—Alex Proyas
April 11, 1994

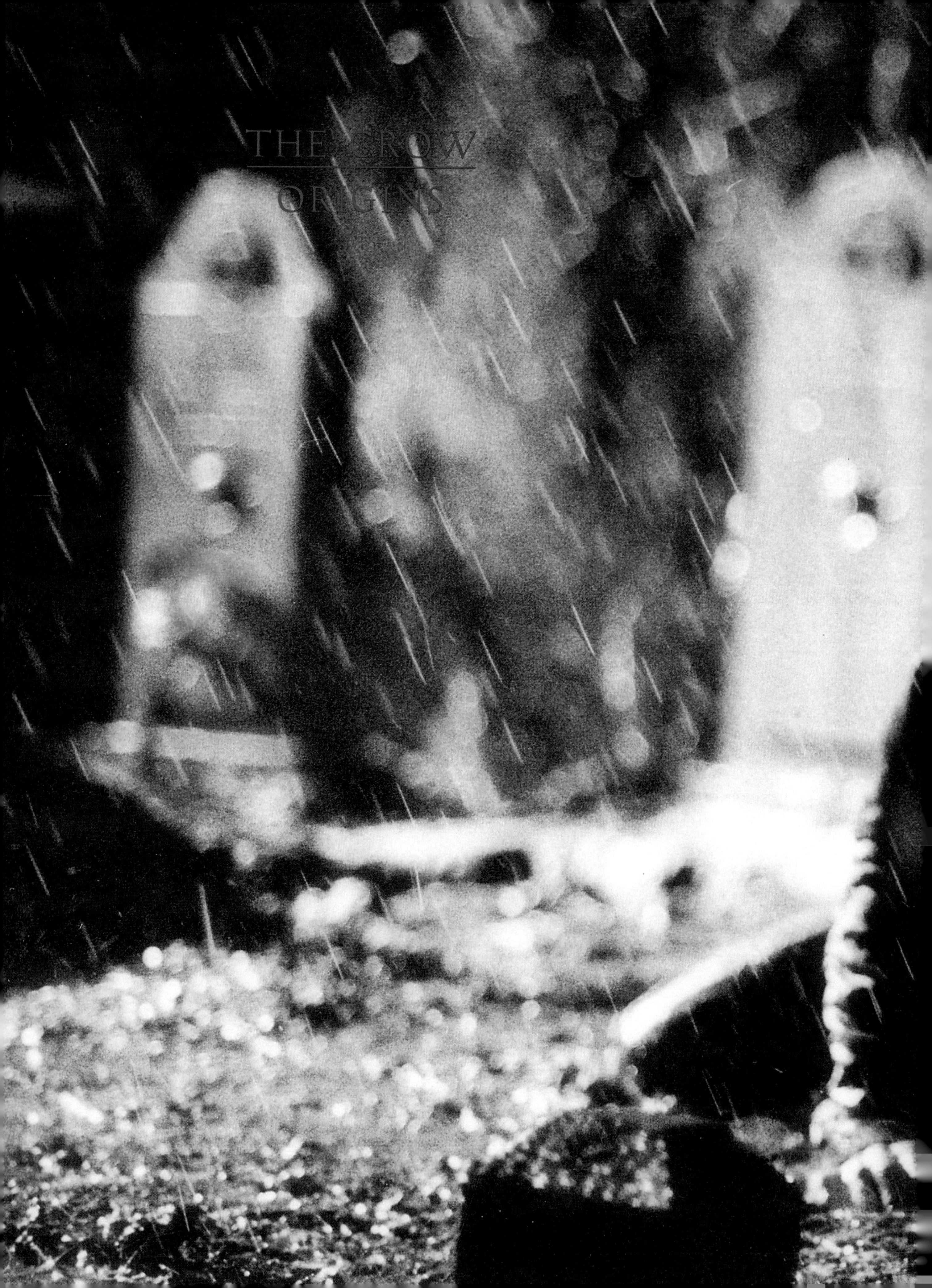
THE CROW
ORIGINS

It all began with James O'Barr's dark saga of love and justice.

O'Barr is no stranger to life's adversities. Born in January of 1960, he grew up in the Detroit area, raised in institutional and foster care. A self-taught artist since his early teens, O'Barr learned his craft through direct observation. He studied Renaissance sculpture, particularly Michelangelo's works, live models, and photographic still lifes.

O'Barr's early comics influence was Frank Frazetta, "just like every other 15-year-old male," he said. "But then I discovered the guys that Frazetta was getting his stuff from, people like N.C. Wyeth and Alex Raymond." Will Eisner, creator of *The Spirit*, most directly influenced O'Barr's earlier work. Eisner's 1940s strip about a wisecracking masked crime fighter was the first to truly bring cinematic visuals into comic storytelling.

"When Warren Publishing brought out their *Spirit* reprints in the seventies, I bought them, but thought they were too cartoony. I was more into The Studio guys like Barry Smith [Windsor-Smith, Jeffrey Jones, Bernie Wrightson and Michael Kaluta all shared a common studio for a time], but later I really studied Eisner closely. Eisner's use of panels is amazing. He really taught me about layout, pacing and story structure. He told complete stories in just eight pages, and they always worked."

O'Barr began *The Crow* in 1981 while he was stationed in Berlin. "I joined the Marines after someone very close to me was killed by a drunk driver. I just wanted to stop thinking about it and have some structure in my life. But, I was still filled with such rage and frustration that I had to get it out before it destroyed me. One day I just began drawing *The Crow*; it came pouring out."

O'Barr heard of another tragedy that helped inspire his final plotline. "It's about a young couple who were killed tragically over an engagement ring. I thought this was totally outlandish, a $30.00 ring, two lives wasted—that became the beginning of the focal point, and the idea that there could be a love so strong that it could transcend death, that it could refuse death and this soul would not rest until it could set things right. My character of Eric is able to return from the grave because some things just cannot be forgiven. In the comic book, he knows what he's there for—he's like a steamroller and there's absolutely nothing that's going to stop him from righting this wrong." *The Crow* dramatizes O'Barr's belief that "an absolute, pure love does exist," and that "there are no boundaries between good and evil where love is concerned."

The first issue of *The Crow* was dedicated to Ian Curtis, lead singer for the art-punk band Joy Division, who hung himself at age 25. "The way Ian Curtis fought through his inadequacy in order to communicate really affected me," said O'Barr. "The band, the content of the songs, I was right on their wavelength. His suicide over his worsening epilepsy just reinforced things even more, since I'm an epileptic myself. In the beginning, I tried to name each chapter after a Joy Division song, but after awhile it became tedious finding ways to make them fit."

The entire storyline of *The Crow* seems to be driven by music. Quotes from rock poet Jim Carroll and lyrics by Robert Smith of The Cure are spread throughout, and even Eric's body movements are inspired by punk icon Iggy Pop. "I started going out to the clubs in Berlin, seeing bands like Bauhaus, Nick Cave and the German industrial groups. When I finally started drawing *The Crow*, I was listening to The Cure and Joy Division almost exclusively. People say that Robert Smith inspired Eric, or they think it was Johnny Depp in *Edward Scissorhands*—but actually, I used Peter Murphy from Bauhaus. Like I said, I'd seen them in the German clubs and thought he was pretty cool; really liked those cheekbones."

Though obviously a part of rock flamboyancy, Eric's mime-like visage was not a tribute to Kiss or Alice Cooper. His makeup is based on Irony from British theater's three faces of

  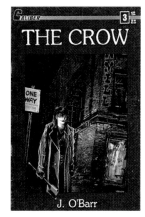 

The first four issues released by Caliber are now hard-to-find and highly collectible.

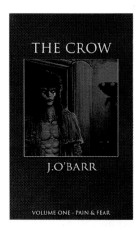
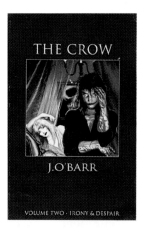
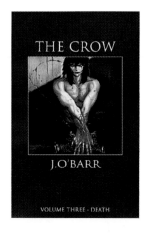
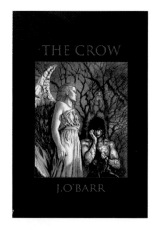

Tundra Publishing released the conclusion in 1992 and Kitchen Sink Press followed with the graphic novel containing the complete story with previously unpublished material.

Drama: Pain, Irony and Despair. If you look carefully you will see these masks hanging in Eric and Shelly's apartment in scenes of the comic book.

After his discharge from the Marines, O'Barr continued his painting and illustration, as well as some scattered comic work, including a short piece in 1987 for Marvel Comics' *Savage Tales*. He supported himself doing a series of odd jobs, including auto-detailing for a Detroit body shop. "I finished the first 40 pages back in '81 and sent photocopies to every publisher I could find. Absolutely no one was interested, which didn't surprise me that much because the thing was so confusing; it didn't start at the beginning and had lots of flashbacks. I hadn't seen anyone doing that at the time, and now I can see why. Presenting a non-linear story in 32-page segments isn't very commercial. So it sat on the shelf for seven years before I showed it to Gary Reed when he was starting up Caliber."

At last the time was right and the first issue of *The Crow* appeared from Caliber Press in February, 1989. The response was immediate and positive.

Four issues were released before financial realities forced the book to go on hiatus in '89. O'Barr had planned to end the series with one more double-sized chapter, *Death*. "I always saw *The Crow* as a fixed story, never a contin-

uing character like in the superhero books." O'Barr turned to the creator of the *Teenage Mutant Ninja Turtles*, Kevin Eastman, and his creator-friendly Tundra Publishing Ltd., to complete the story. With a reputation for first-class production values, Tundra decided to repackage the out-of-print and still in demand Caliber comics into two high-quality collections. The third graphic novel would contain the unpublished conclusion in the same lush format. "The first Tundra book came out in early 1991," said O'Barr, "and I had drawn the last 64 pages in 1990. They wanted to stagger the first two volumes in order to build interest for the final book, so I had a year and a half to go back and tinker with my artwork. I ended up redrawing and rewriting large chunks; pulling back on the violence, and adding more flashbacks, trying to make the story more understandable and the character more sympathetic."

Unlike other gore-drenched comics, *The Crow*'s scenes of mayhem are balanced with flashback sequences of the characters Eric and Shelly in happier times. Such a pure love existed between them—before it was cruelly snuffed out by urban street thugs—that Eric returns from the grave to find justice and hunt down the gang that murdered him and his fiancée.

O'Barr explained, "With every one of the people who perpetrated the crime against

him and his fiancée, he is erasing his reason for being. The closer he gets to the five killers, the less reason for his existence, and he can finally be with Shelly."

Death, the final chapter of *The Crow*, was released in May of 1992 and became the best-selling single issue in Tundra Publishing's history.

In 1993, Kitchen Sink Press, Inc. acquired *The Crow* and released the three single issues as a 244-page graphic novel containing the complete story, unpublished art and an 8-page color gallery. Finally O'Barr's decade-old dream was fully realized.

"I don't believe Eric is a hero. He can be absolutely cold-blooded and ruthless at times. When he goes into a room to get one person, everyone else in the room is probably going to die as well. I think what he's doing is terribly romantic, but I wouldn't call him a hero."

—James O'Barr,
creator of *The Crow*

The response to James O'Barr's brooding and violent tale of love,

loss and retribution was near instantaneous, attracting the attention of mostly older readers, college-age and above: a non-superhero crowd. It wasn't long before Hollywood took notice.

Around the time the second issue hit the stands, O'Barr was approached by a young genre director with an offer to buy the rights to his creation. "It was basically a one-time, lump sum for everything," said O'Barr. "All rights, all media, in perpetuity; but the money was pretty good, considering. I was going to do it. I figured it was a long shot at best that anything would ever come of it. Hell, I was doing autobody work. I'd be a fool not to take the money." But on the strenuous advice of friends, O'Barr finally consulted a Hollywood agent who quickly told him to hold onto his copyrights and not sell himself short. It was good advice.

At this same time, mid-1989, "cyberpunk" writer John Shirley was contacting Caliber about his own project. "I had a comic story called "Angry Angels," which was like a *High Plains Drifter* riff but set in the inner-city," Shirley recalled. "So I called them up and pitched it on the phone, and they said that my thing sounded like their book, *The Crow.* They sent me the first two issues and I read those and thought, 'This should be a movie.'"

Shirley had lived the street-level music lifestyle with a vengeance, fronting bands with names like Sado-Nation and Panther Moderns. He had also recorded an album for the Celluloid label in Paris, appropriately titled *Obsession.* He honed his music-informed, street conscious style of fiction by hacking out a few of the *Executioner*-like *Traveler* novels, using the name D. B. Drumm. Later, he created the more original *Specialist* series, which he wrote under the name John Cutter.

"In 1984 I moved to Los Angeles," related Shirley, "and had three novels come out in 1988, but I was still broke all the time, scraping by doing television scripts." Typically, the sudden cancellation of ABC's *Max Headroom* meant that his work for the innovative show was never even produced. "Since my own writing wasn't selling as well as I wanted, I started looking for other story properties I could develop into film projects. Weirder things have happened."

When he read *The Crow*, Shirley had an immediate response to O'Barr's many musical and literary references, which reflected many of his own influences and touchstones. "I felt it had been written about my people, my friends; from the streetcreep scumbags to the French imagist poet—the overt music passages. It all made sense to me."

THE PRODUCERS

Shirley met up-and-coming producer Jeff Most through the bass player in John's band. At that time, Most was enrolled in NYU film school's dramatic writing program and was active in the underground film and music scenes. In 1983, he, like Shirley, moved to Los Angeles, where he soon began producing music video programs for syndication. The two met again and quickly became partners when Most optioned Shirley's *The Specialist* eleven-novel series.

"John had this closet full of books and I noticed the *The Specialist* books in there," recalled Most. "He didn't want to admit he wrote them at first. I felt they'd make a great action film and optioned them immediately, even though I had no money at that point."

When Shirley showed Most his two issues of *The Crow*, he had a similar instant reaction. "What really turned me on to the character was that he was not the typical, cookie-cutter hero," said Most. "This is a guy who recites poetry and is motivated by an intense love and passion. He's a lot like Frankenstein's monster; he has this humanity balanced out by this ruthlessness and need for revenge. I knew I had to get it made."

Shirley contacted O'Barr through a mutual friend in Detroit. Just as issue three of *The*

Left to right: Creator of *The Crow* James O'Barr, Producer Jeff Most

Crow was coming out in late 1989, Shirley brought him together with Most. "Their enthusiasm convinced me that the film would be done correctly," said O'Barr. "Even though it was for far less money than I had previously been offered, I wasn't selling out my copyright, and it was the best chance of the film turning out to be something I'd want to see. I just went with my instincts."

The deal done, Shirley immediately began writing treatments while Most started making contacts with studios and established producers. But how to adapt O'Barr's vision to a film?

One of the first hurdles was the fact that O'Barr's final installment of *The Crow* had yet to appear. "We didn't know how James was going to handle the ending," recalled Most. "It was an odd situation for us to be in, but we didn't let a detail like that stop us from moving ahead with it."

From the very beginning Most wanted to downplay the drug use in the comic while stressing the love story. "What Eric does to avenge his and Shelly's death is extremely violent, but it's also very romantic, and the pain and suffering he goes through is very real," said Most. "But I just couldn't have him running around shooting morphine into his neck like in the comic. Even for an anti-hero it was too much."

Other basic changes to O'Barr's work included making the crow "familiar" a real bird, not just a symbol for Eric's conscience and sanity. "And having Eric follow the crow, a real bird, which other characters could also react to, just had better possibilities for action and visuals," remembered Most. Thus, with the crow acting as a guide, it was also decided that Eric would be suffering from a memory loss. "We wanted the audience to find out Eric's mission at the same time he did, making it a quest for knowledge as well as retribution."

O'Barr's original rock music influences were always a central concern. "Making Eric a guitarist as a way to tie in more music in a logical manner was a decision right from the start," recalled Most. In fact, many early versions of the script would cite specific songs during certain scenes.

In December, 1989, with treatment and comics in hand, Jeff Most continued to shop the project around Hollywood. "There was some interest, but mostly people didn't understand it, or were even openly hostile," said Most. "Only Ed Pressman really saw the material's true potential."

Independent producer Edward R. Pressman has been considered an oasis of quality in the film industry for over twenty-five years, specializing in personal, artist-driven projects.

Among the 40-plus films to his credit are significant debut features for a wealth of young or first-time directors, such as Terrence Malick (*Badlands*), Oliver Stone (*The Hand*), and Brian DePalma (*Sisters*). Pressman often provided an outlet for notable foreign directors as well; filmmakers like Wolfgang Petersen (*Das Boot*), Fred Schepisi (*Plenty*) and the Taviani Brothers (*Good Morning, Babylon*).

Pressman is also no stranger to pop culture fare, having produced *Conan the Barbarian*, as well as the satire *Crimewave* (with Sam Raimi and Joel & Ethan Cohen).

"It was something that I was immediately attracted to," said Pressman about *The Crow*. "It went a step beyond the usual comic book movie. I saw in O'Barr's work a unique film as visually stunning as Frazetta's world for *Conan*; and to see a whole universe is something that is obviously ideal for movies, and the best movies—certainly in the fantasy areas—are ones that have you experience something that you've never experienced before. I knew, however, that it would need exactly the right script, director and star to make it work." By December of 1990, Pressman and Most had a deal, and Shirley was attached as first writer.

As his senior vice-president of production, Caldecot "Cotty" Chubb was Edward Pressman's point man for the development of THE CROW, shepherding Shirley's initial drafts of the screenplay. Chubb had been with Pressman for several years, receiving executive producer credit on such films as *Good Morning, Babylon*, *To Sleep with Anger*, and *Hoffa*.

"I did numerous treatments and then three full drafts," said Shirley. "They kept saying Eric was too invulnerable, had no true adversary with real power. It was my idea to give him the Achilles' heel of shooting the crow to hurt Eric. The flashes of memory when he touches somebody were an explication device, but also previewed what his power might be."

THE DIRECTOR

In March, 1991, after months of meetings, treatments, notes and preliminary versions, Shirley delivered a draft that was solid enough to attract Pressman's first choice for director, Alex Proyas.

"I think it's always a matter of matching the property to the filmmaker," stated Pressman. "Most of the films I've gotten involved with have been through the filmmaker first and then the property. But occasionally, as with *Conan* and with THE CROW, it was the opposite. But I think it was not till I met Alex Proyas and got to know him and his work that I saw the perfect match and saw that there was a movie."

Australian Alex Proyas was a director widely known in the commercial and rock video milieu, directing unique spots for Coca-Cola and Nike, and strikingly original music videos for Sting, Joe Jackson and INXS. "I was just waiting for [a project] that had a little bit of something different going for it," said Proyas. "There was a lot of stuff that I was offered, things that really seemed straight to me, really linear, and they were all genre pieces, all kind of predictable." Indeed, Alex was very much in demand in Hollywood, but his "day job" afforded him the luxury of being able to choose his American debut feature very carefully. Then came THE CROW.

"When I was shown the comic by the producers, I'd heard of it, but I'd never seen it before," said Proyas. "What I liked about it is this: it starts with elements where you think you know what direction they're going to head in, and then it gets totally twisted off those rails; that appeals to me—anything that does something unexpected. And it's about characters in very intense situations, which is always great. It's the stuff that drama is made of."

As Proyas signed on, more drafts from Shirley followed in July and August of 1991. Two pivotal scenes from the comic that were to remain virtually unchanged through all drafts were the sequence at Gideon's pawnshop and

Eric's uninvited visit to Funboy and Darla when they are shooting up. Eric quips a joke taken from the comic book, and preaches to Darla that "Mother is the name for God in the lips and hearts of all children."

Shirley still had the crow speak telepathically to Eric. Sarah is much like "Ellie" in the comic, a very young girl with a drug-addicted mother, Darla, only now she also had an older brother, Denny, who has been seduced by the streets. A mysterious "spirit guardian," who recognizes Eric's supernatural powers and attempts to explain them, was also created.

O'Barr felt the creative team was going too far afield from his original concept. "I wrote a ten-page outline explaining everything—all the characters' motives, what they did for a living, that type of thing. Something to help them stay on track."

A decision was then made to have a second writer take a pass at the material. Award-

Left to right: Executive Producer Robert L. Rosen, Director Alex Proyas, Producer Edward R. Pressman, Co-Producer Caldecot Chubb

winning horror fiction writer David J. Schow had done work for New Line Cinema on the syndicated television program *Freddy's Nightmares*, as well as several features, including *Leatherface: Texas Chainsaw Massacre III*, and *Critters 3 & 4*. It was during this period that Schow wrote a "spec" script, *Dead Reckoning*, designed as "an action horror film," which brought him to the attention of Cotty Chubb. He called Schow in August of 1991 to attend a group meeting at Pressman's headquarters.

"My initial feeling was that there were too many bad guys in the comic," said Schow. "We needed to single out the worst ones, differentiate them, and put them in some sort of hierarchy that we could follow as Eric tracked them down. I remember that when I told Ed Pressman that what he was really looking for was a 'Gothic, rock and roll Terminator,' Ed just lit right up. Bringing in Devil's Night was at first just to give the villains a more esoteric agenda; that plan became more nihilistic as we sought to steer their motivations away from the predictable, conventional bad-guy stuff. It also conveniently localized the film to Detroit and anchored it in reality, since fires have been set through Detroit on Devil's Night every year going back ten or twelve years."

"The first script that was shown to me really was something that was not what the comic was," said Proyas. "We spent a lot of time really bringing it right back to the flavor of the comic book." 'Make it darker,' became the watchwords for THE CROW. Urban decay, squalor, drugs, poverty, crime, and above all, a sense of hopelessness and moral outrage that could make the tiniest elements of brightness shine more significantly. Gradually, the central conflict of the film coalesced around the parallel triumvirates of Eric, Albrecht the cop, and Sarah, the little girl, versus Top Dollar, the malevolent crime lord, his Asian half-sister Myca (whose mystic bent—or bent mysticism—allows her to divine Eric's true nature), and Grange, Top Dollar's lieutenant.

Officer Albrecht was put at the scene of Eric's murder, where he forms a bond with Sarah, now reconceived as a skatepunk street kid, a bit older, and the only child of the drugged-out Darla. Various other semi-mystical or supernatural characters were conceived, developed, then abandoned. Albrecht, who had originally sacrificed his life for Eric at the climax, was permitted to survive. Sarah was given a surrogate parent/sister relationship with Eric's murdered fiancée, Shelly. It was decided, contrary to the comic, that Eric comes out of his grave with only the sense he must follow the crow...which leads him to items, places and people that can trigger the return of bursts of memory (via flashback through physical contact).

"The writing and rewriting became almost constant," said Schow, and by March, 1992, the skeleton of THE CROW was solid enough for the production to secure a "negative pick-up" deal with Paramount Studios. The long-established practice of negative pick-up has many variations, but essentially, it allows the studios to release pictures they probably wouldn't have made otherwise, which in turn keeps canny producers like Pressman and Most in business. The majors—who are best suited for making glossy, star-driven, high-concept movies—need a steady stream of product to keep their distribution pipelines (and revenue streams) flowing smoothly; they also need to continuously supply theatres with fresh product.

Next, a start date for principal photography had to be locked down, and locations for filming chosen. The clockwork of business began to grind while revisions continued. "I ended up going down to Australia in May of 1992," said Schow, "just to work more closely with Alex. We labored over this monster at his house, my house, in hotels, at Pressman Studios, everywhere—and by that fall we looked at each other and said, 'you know, we've been doing this for a year.'"

THE STAR

"We considered various musicians, people with an interesting look," said Jeff Most. Texas rocker Charlie Sexton was one such case. "I loved his cheekbones," recalled O'Barr. "I always saw Eric as having really high cheekbones, like Peter Murphy's. I heard that Charlie's Texas drawl was just too strong for a story set in Detroit."

The budding action star Brandon Lee was ultimately the first choice by both producers. Pressman commented, "We had considered some more established actors and we were concerned that certain of these actors did not have the athletic ability. Other people had the athletic ability but not the acting talents. Brandon combined it all. When Brandon walked into this office, it was an immediate flash. We knew we had our Eric Draven that instant."

"The fans of this comic book are very vocal
and extremely involved with this character...
it moves them and Brandon has brought
[Eric] to life, which is no small job."

—Producer Jeff Most

Brandon Lee was the son of legendary film icon Bruce Lee

and his wife Linda, who is of Scandinavian descent. He was born on February 1st, 1965, in Oakland, California. Brandon recounted his years in Hong Kong to interviewer Jennifer Peters: "My dad wanted me to train in martial arts and he started training me himself, literally as soon as I could walk—when I was two, one and a half. My dad originated a style that's called *jeet kune do*. He trained me in this style while he was alive."

After his father's untimely death at age 32, Brandon, his sister, and mother went to live in Los Angeles. He told reporter Caroline Hambrick: "I had a very normal childhood. After my father passed away, my mother was responsible for moving us out of the limelight as a very conscious act on her part. And I thank her for it very much because it did just that—it gave us a normal childhood. I never wanted another one."

It seems from the very beginning, Brandon was drawn towards performing. "Since my earliest memories, I always wanted to be an actor, and I pursued that from the time I was very young," Brandon told interviewer Wilson Goodson while on the set of THE CROW. "I have really never felt that there were other paths for me. It is all I have ever wanted to do. My father was a martial artist first and that was his passion. That was what made him what he was, and he was an actor second. Not that he wasn't a very good actor, just that it was not his primary concern. To the degree that my father put his passions and his energies into the martial arts, I would only hope to be able to invest as much passion into acting."

After the usual high school drama classes, Brandon left to attend acting classes with Lee Strasberg, later going on to study acting at Emerson College in Boston, Massachusetts. Brandon next joined Eric Morris' American New Theater company in New York City. He followed the company's relocation to Los Angeles and appeared in their production of *Full Fed Beast* for playwright John Lee Hancock (Hancock later wrote Clint Eastwood's *A Perfect World*).

Brandon returned to training at the Inosanto Academy of Martial Arts in Marina Del Rey, California, which was run by two of Bruce Lee's foremost students and instructors, Danny Inosanto and Ted Wong. Brandon described Bruce Lee's martial arts training and philosophy to interviewer Caroline Vie: "My father just mixed several existing techniques to find a style of his own. He used to say that he was using everything essential in each and every technique to get a very personal way of fighting."

At Inosanto's *dojo*, Brandon met fellow student Jeff Imada. He was impressed by the younger Lee's spirit and good humor. The two became close friends, and Jeff later served as Brandon's stunt coordinator and collaborator on fight choreography.

On being the son of the martial arts legend, Brandon told Rachel Hambrick: "Well, there isn't much negative. Sometimes it can be personally difficult, but I'd imagine that everyone has personal problems, you know? Professionally, I can't pretend that it's anything except a positive thing. I believe it has certainly created opportunity for me that I would not have had as quickly, were I not Bruce Lee's son." Brandon told Vie: "I don't think my father would have liked his life accomplishments to become a burden upon his son's shoulders. It took me a few years to understand that, but once I got it, I didn't let myself be overwhelmed by Bruce Lee's personality nor his fame."

Brandon made several appearances on Hong Kong television with his father, but his first professional acting job came at age twenty, when he appeared in the CBS television film *Kung Fu: The Movie* (1986), which was the full-length pilot for the series *Kung Fu: The Next Generation*. He played the long lost and revengeful son of David Carradine's character Caine. Brandon next took on the role of the evil son of a Yakuza godfather on an episode of *O'Hara* with Pat Morita.

It bothered Brandon that Asian actors were not consistently getting starring roles in American films and television. He confided to Wilson Goodson: "The fact of the matter is that when my dad was over here, during the years he was doing *The Green Hornet*, he

eventually had to go to Hong Kong to pursue his acting career." This was thirty years ago, when there were no Asian leading men working in either film or television. "There is *still* not a Chinese leading man in America—not one. There are some very fine actors, but no leading men, no one somebody would bank a film on who is Asian."

Brandon himself had to travel to Hong Kong in order to make his feature film debut, starring in *Legacy of Rage* (1988). Made by D & B Films, a rough and tumble purveyor of action product, his character is betrayed by a friend and takes the rap for a mobster's murder. Though he spoke fluent Cantonese at the time, Brandon's voice is dubbed in the film, which is standard practice for these quickly made assembly-line productions.

You may find *Legacy of Rage* in Chinese-language video and laserdisc stores, with which Brandon was obviously familiar, telling interviewer Jennifer Peters: "I have quite a [video] library at home. I've never been that big on the stuff that comes out of the United States. It's really so simple compared to the stuff they do in Hong Kong. I love John Woo's movies, I'd love to work with him. Hong Kong directors are the best in the world as far as action scenes are concerned."

Brandon's next film was the espionage thriller, *Laser Mission* (1990). Filmed in Namibia with featured star Ernest Borgnine, this low budget production managed to be both earnest and goofy at the same time. Brandon played likeable spy Michael Gold, with crusty Borgnine playing a laser weapons expert. When the world is imperiled, Brandon must sort things out with a blonde 'patootie' claiming to be the professor's daughter. You can tell Brandon is having fun with the part, rising far above the clichéd material.

The following year Brandon finally made his American feature film debut in *Showdown in Little Tokyo* for Warner Brothers. He played a policeman combating a new wave of intervention in L.A.'s Little Tokyo by the Yakuza, Japan's organized crime syndicate. His unlikely partner Kenner, played by Dolph Lundgren, had a personal stake in the case and Johnny, played by Brandon, must keep him on the right side of the law. Again, Brandon outshone the material and established himself as a credible screen presence in the domestic market.

It wasn't long before Brandon landed a major starring role, that of Jake Lo in *Rapid Fire* for 20th Century Fox, written with Brandon in mind. He played an orphan who must come to terms with the death of his father who was killed in the Tienanmen Square massacre. A grizzled cop, played by Powers Booth, is in charge of protecting Jake after he witnesses a mob murder. A tentative father/son relationship develops between the two. Brandon identified with the role: "Jake is struggling to come to grips with the relationship with his father, which is something I've butted my head against many times."

Brandon worked with Jeff Imada on *Rapid Fire*'s fight choreography to bring some Hong Kong movie flair to the film. He recalled to Wilson Goodson: "I simply felt that [Jake Lo] was a young man who was a highly-trained martial artist, but someone very much like myself, or most people, who is not accustomed to finding himself in violent life or death situations. This, once again, was an aspect of his character that had to be shown in the choreography. He was mostly out just to survive, to preserve his own life. Given an opportunity in any situation, he would certainly just as soon run, or get away from the conflict, because it was not a conflict of his choosing."

The fight scenes were made more natural by logically incorporating the setting into the sequence. "I always like to use what the environment has," said Imada, "so you're not preventing yourself from getting full use of the set. I've always been taught to use what's around you. Whether it's a newspaper or a plate or a door—anything to give the fighter an edge. It's what you should actually do in combat."

Brandon was very happy with the results of his work with Jeff Imada, telling Goodson: "It was a particularly rewarding experience because I had never experienced anything like it before, seeing something that we were involved with, thinking up the scenes and then seeing them realized the way we had imagined them." Brandon's power and screen presence made *Rapid Fire* a popular action film, above the usual pedestrian level for films of this sort. 20th Century Fox signed Brandon to do two more films for the studio.

Fox wasn't the only one to recognize Brandon's potential; Ed Pressman also put Brandon on his roster. "We signed him for three pictures. The last time we signed an actor for a multiple picture deal was when we signed Schwarzenegger for *Conan the Barbarian*," said THE CROW producer. "We saw the same potential. I think there's a grace in Brandon's movements and a power; THE CROW was a perfect vehicle for his strengths."

Production on the film began February 1, 1993, Brandon's 28th birthday. Final shooting in Eric and Shelly's apartment had been saved for the last week, allowing Brandon to work without makeup. On the night of March 31st, he was injured while filming on the loft set at Carolco Studios. A tip from a "dummy round" (a prop bullet that has no gunpowder) had lodged in a gun and was subsequently ejected from the barrel (like a piece of shrapnel) when a blank cartridge was fired. Brandon died hours later at the Wilmington Hospital.

The production immediately shut down while the filmmakers came to grips with the tragedy and tried to figure out what was next. Except for some flashback sequences, the entire story of THE CROW had been filmed by the time of the accident. The question of whether or not the film could be finished was never a technical one, but psychological. "It was unbearable," recalled Pressman. "The first reaction from Alex was that we couldn't go on. There was nothing left. It was all over.

"And then members of the cast and crew got together and all said that we had to continue, the performance itself was done and Brandon was so proud," Pressman continued. "I felt compelled to finish this work to preserve Brandon's legacy, the incredible performance he'd given."

Brandon saw the role of Eric Draven as his breakthrough role, one that would lift him from the martial arts film world. He always thought of himself as an actor first and spoke of how versatile he wanted to become. Brandon wanted to do the big budget studio films, but also smaller intimate ones. THE CROW can easily be seen as the perfect vehicle for his aspirations, since it straddles the worlds of action films and romance. Brandon stated, "Eric's trying to come back to take vengeance on something that was done to him and the woman he loves. It's a very personal story."

Brandon felt a deep commitment to keeping the roots of the film deep in its origin: "I read the script first, but the comic book is wonderful. It's a very pure work. The artist has been on the set a lot and I've gotten to meet him. You wouldn't necessarily bring him home to meet your mother, I think he'd like me to say that, but it really is a very pure work. It came from some personal experiences of his own. The interesting thing is that it's essentially a love story of a man and a woman who are vic-

tims of a terrible crime, and he gets a chance to come back and try to seek justice, which is something that, when you read the news or just look around, does not happen. It's very satisfying in that way. After the script was written, Alex [Proyas] and I went back to the comic book and tried to find the beats of the story that didn't make it into the script."

It can be said Brandon was an actor who wanted to be involved in every aspect of the filmmaking process. He felt responsible for the film, and director Alex Proyas was willing to work with him. Brandon also asked for the removal of one of the characters from the script that he thought was a stereotype. "From his first involvement," Proyas said, "Brandon was specific about his thoughts and a lot of his ideas were incorporated. There is no doubt that Brandon's talents were many and varied. I was constantly amazed at his grasp of film from every possible perspective, and without a doubt it was he who defined his character, even at the script stage. He contributed a great deal to the finished film, far beyond what is expected from an actor in any normal situation. I feel we collaborated in a much more real sense than in most actor/director relationships. More than anyone involved in the film, Brandon was my sounding board regarding many aspects of the film, even scenes that didn't involve his character."

Brandon's character, Eric Draven, is endowed with supernatural abilities, but his emotions and reactions are those of a very sensitive and human person. Jon Polito, who plays Gideon, the sleazy pawnshop owner, tapped into this conception of the character when he talked about acting with Brandon. "Eric wasn't a vicious person until his death; he was forced into it. There was a parallel between Brandon and his character; a truly sweet guy who takes on darkness. Brandon was sort of a gentle soul, but when I was acting with him, I could really feel the tremendous amount of power he threw across a room."

In an interview on the set, Brandon spoke of the makeup that Eric Draven applies as being necessary for him to make the transformation to carry out his quest. "I think it is just his reaction to being pushed to the limit of his tolerance. He perhaps finds that he cannot deal with what is going on, and by assuming this character he creates someone who can."

Sofia Shinas, who plays Shelly Webster, laughed and spoke of how different Brandon looked coming on the set for the flashback sequences. "He would be all clean and serene, but Eric was still the same person when he returned to avenge Shelly's murder and his own. The truly amazing thing about the film is how very poignant it is—what Brandon did with the role, especially because

he is in makeup. We are always aware of Eric's pain and his motivation."

Ernie Hudson, who plays Officer Albrecht, commented, "I was very touched by the fact that Brandon's spirit, his warmth, and his heart came through. And he essentially made it a love story. When I first got involved, all I saw was the dark side. All I saw was the violence. But when I saw the movie, what came through for me was the love story. At the end, I know that they hadn't shot most of the love scenes and the scenes dealing with his personal relationship with the girl. It still came through because of his performance and what he brought to the role; it came through loud and clear."

Brandon talked about how playing Eric and reflecting on the character could make you think more deeply about the things in your life you take for granted. He quoted a passage from Paul Bowles' *Sheltering Sky*:

"Because we do not know when we will die we get to think of life as an inexhaustible well and yet everything happens only a certain number of times and a very small number really. How many more times will you remember a certain afternoon of your childhood, an afternoon that is so deeply a part of your life that you can't even conceive of your life without it. Perhaps four or five times more? Perhaps not even that. How many times will you watch the full moon rise, perhaps twenty, and yet it all seems so limitless."

This is a notion that Brandon carried into the film in a scene he improvised with Ernie Hudson. "That's why I love the way Brandon ended the scene," Hudson said. "It wasn't in the script. Eric picks up the picture and says, 'Who's this?' and Albrecht says, 'It's my wife but we are getting a divorce.' Eric tells him about Shelly and it's a very strong moment which tells you to value the life you have."

An allegory about love, loss and retribution, THE CROW is a modern urban fable with Eric Draven coming back from the grave to help the living and avenge the dead. There is a clear division of good and evil, but all the "good" characters have their own personal devils.

Ernie Hudson, who portrays Officer Albrecht in the film, was born in Michigan and graduated from the Yale School of Drama. He received a Dramalogue award for his Los Angeles performance in *The Great White Hope* and has since appeared in the films *Ghostbusters*, *The Hand That Rocks the Cradle*, and *No Escape*, as well as *Tribeca* and *Wild Palms* for television.

"In '88," recalled Hudson, "I was working on a series and Brandon came by because he was friends with Miguel Ferrer. He was very young then. I was impressed when we got together to do THE CROW with how much he'd grown and matured. We confided in each other and shared things. I think for the scene in the apartment, we drew on our conversations."

Originally intended to take place on the street outside the police headquarters, the intimate scene between Eric and Albrecht was moved to the officer's home, so the audience could learn more about him. Recently demoted to a beat cop, at odds with his superiors, and over-whelmed by crime in the streets, somehow his encounter with Eric gives Officer Albrecht renewed hope.

"Once we were in the apartment the scene really changed," said Hudson. "What came out was how Eric and Albrecht were kindred spirits. Sometimes life can be great and you think you've got it together, and other times it's all a big mess. Albrecht was at that point in his life. Part of it had to do with him being horrified by what had happened to that girl; he had gone to the hospital with her and his life was never quite the same again. Albrecht was very low and Eric helps give him focus."

The relationship Hudson developed with Brandon offscreen helped to create the tone of gentle humor that characterizes their scenes together. The bond between Eric Draven and Sarah is also well established in the film. Rochelle Davis said acting with Brandon always seemed genuine. "I did one scene with him where he made me cry," she said during a break on the set. "I, sort of, know how to make myself cry a little bit, but it's better when it's real."

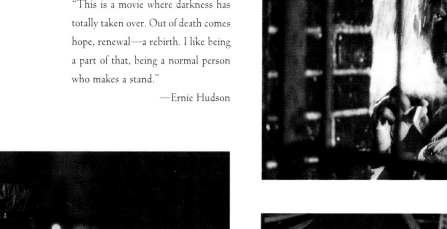

"This is a movie where darkness has totally taken over. Out of death comes hope, renewal—a rebirth. I like being a part of that, being a normal person who makes a stand."

—Ernie Hudson

THE CROW was Rochelle Davis' first role and the film owes a lot to her performance in terms of the depths of emotion that she pulls from the audience. Her feelings always seem authentic. She said Brandon was always there to help her. "He's great to work with. He's really easy to work with; very lovable, very sweet."

Director Alex Proyas praises Davis: "Rochelle is really a terrific actor. She has to take all the credit for her performance. I saw my role as trying to make her comfortable enough with the material to just do her thing, be as natural as possible. Fortunately this seemed easy for her."

Davis, however, does give Proyas some credit: "He helped me a lot. If I messed up—I messed up a couple of times on my skateboarding—he didn't have a fit. I mean, I was all upset and worked up and he just said, 'Oh, it's okay. We'll do it again, just take a rest for a minute.' If I was doing a scene and he noticed I was lost and didn't know what I was doing, he'd tell me, 'What I'm trying to do here is…' and if I didn't understand, tell me again in better words until I understood."

The story is as much Sarah's as it is Eric's, especially with Davis' narration creating lyrical bookends for the film. "A lot of her and Eric's friendship is that she needed somebody like a parent. Eric and Shelly are like her family, the closest people she has to her because her own mom is on drugs and messed up a lot," said Davis.

Shelly Webster, Eric Draven's fiancée, is played by Sofia Shinas, an actor and singer with extensive stage experience. Like Davis, THE CROW is her first film. She had ample pressure put upon her due to the fact that her character's death is the terrible sadness that compels Eric's actions. Said Sofia, "This is

why he returns. It is his mission—taking care of business so that he can be with Shelly in the afterlife, and they will live on some other plane happily ever after."

Proyas gave her and Brandon the time and space needed to play with their characters and make discoveries during rehearsals. This technique resulted in a spontaneous feeling in their performances in the flashback scenes of better days. "We had the script before us, but we also improvised," said Shinas. "Brandon wanted to make sure that the audience had a tremendous amount of empathy for Eric, and Alex was very supportive of our explorations. Brandon and I were both so excited and we wanted to make sure that we did this properly. Alex was very dedicated and worked really hard to help us understand exactly what he wanted, to bring forth new emotions." Added the director, Proyas: "You could make an entire film about love and not get it right."

A lot of the people in the film are bad. They are a very entertaining bunch of characters. I wanted them to have a lot of depth and was looking for very good actors who could provide that. I gave them some humor so that you hate them, but you also enjoy what they are like as people.

—Director Alex Proyas

"Bad people out on the street tonight," says Officer Albrecht, watching as T-Bird and his hoodlum crew roll by Maxi-Dogs. Seconds later, another fiery explosion rips through the night. Top Dollar rules this particular section of hell from atop his nightclub lair, Club Trash. When not smoking eyeballs with his half-sister/lover, Myca, he directs a network of badass criminals; his master plan has more to do with existential angst than with illegal commerce. "Greed is for amateurs. Disorder, chaos, anarchy—now that's fun," Top Dollar tells his troops.

Michael Wincott creates a fascinating and novel villain. His sinister deadpan delivery personifies evil while walking the line between scary and humorous. A graduate of Julliard, Wincott has appeared on television in episodes of *The Equalizer* and *Miami Vice*; on stage in *The Secret Rapture* and *Talk Radio*; and on film in *Born on the Fourth of July*, *The Doors*, *Robin Hood: Prince of Thieves*, and *The Three Musketeers*. But it was in Ridley Scott's *1492: Conquest of Paradise* that James O'Barr first noticed him. "They asked me early on if I had any casting suggestions," said the comic creator. "I'd just seen Wincott steal the show from Gerard DePardieu and thought he'd make a great Top Dollar. I was really surprised when they actually got him."

Top Dollar's half sister and equally sadistic lover Myca, is played by Bai Ling. Admittedly very photogenic, she looks quite comfortable handling her role in the film. From the age of fourteen, she was a soldier in the Chinese army in Tibet. Though well-known in her homeland, Bai Ling had been in the United States for two years before getting a chance to be a featured player. She appeared in an episode of the acclaimed TV series *Homicide: Life on the Street*, and is set to star in the Broadway production of *Sansho the Bailiff* to be directed by Andrez Wadja (*Badlands*). "I've played a lot of characters," the young actress stated, "but I have never played one like Myca. She's mean; mean and evil."

"Grange is a corporate killer, an assassin who enjoys what he's doing. He's not a henchman, he doesn't do it reluctantly. He likes investigating the nature of death. He enjoys it."

—Tony Todd

Grange's power as Top Dollar's lieutenant and private assassin is apparent. He may appear to be a shadowy background character, but don't forget he is the one who grabs Sarah and shoots the crow to render Eric vulnerable. Tony Todd gained experience in supernatural horror while starring opposite Virginia Madsen in *Candyman*. He had his film debut in Oliver Stone's *Platoon* and from there can be seen in *Bird*, *Colors*, *Excessive Force*, and *Lean on Me*. Additionally, he has had recurring roles on *Star Trek: The Next Generation* and *Jake and the Fatman*.

"Grange is a corporate killer," said Todd of his character. "He's an assassin who enjoys what he's doing. He's not a henchman, he doesn't do it reluctantly. He likes investigating the nature of death. He enjoys it." Todd explained, "Grange is a strange guy. I didn't really have a fix on him until I discovered this piece [indicating jointed silver finger-cuff]. It looks simple enough, but it was the thing I needed that added a little comic book element."

Top Dollar, Myca and Grange form a triumvirate of evil which parallels the forces of good represented by Eric, Sarah and Albrecht. It's no coincidence that in the climactic battle in the church, Grange battles Albrecht, Myca holds and binds Sarah, and Top Dollar challenges Eric to a jousting match on the roof. The street-level criminals—T-Bird, Skank, Funboy and Tin-Tin—do not have the omniscient power of Top Dollar, but the senseless randomness of their violence conveys its own form of terror.

David Patrick Kelly, who plays T-Bird, studied at the International School of Mime of Marcel Marceau, and worked with renowned acting teacher Mira Rostova. He made his film debut in *The Warriors* and has since been in *48 Hours*, *Commando*, *Dreamscape*, *Malcolm X*, *Wild at Heart*, and on television in *Twin Peaks*.

"The things that inspired me to create T-Bird were based in the 'Revolt of Angels' in John Milton's *Paradise Lost*," Kelly confided during filming. "The concepts of light and dark, and why evil comes in, and the powers of ambition and greed, and the seven deadly sins; these evil things are completely dwarfed by the goodness that avenges them." In fact, T-Bird is quoting Milton to Shelly during

the flashback sequences. Kelly bought an antique copy of *Paradise Lost* specifically for the scene. That this demented pyromaniac can recite poetry with conviction only makes T-Bird that much more chilling.

He again quotes Milton while bound helplessly to the seat of his car by Eric. "He doesn't understand that this is an avenging angel who represents something that goes so far beyond any concept that he has, any value that he accepts. So when he finally does, that's the cathartic moment in the film for this character. The goal is to show that there's something that goes beyond greed, power, money, sex; what they consider power in this world."

The strong bond between the bad guys and T-Bird seems to keep the gang together and their relationship is a close one. It's the strange duality of these killers that they still seem to care about each other. Skank may be sniveling and vicious, yet his genuine mourning for T-Bird is quite touching.

Angel David, who plays Skank, has appeared in a number of New York based stage productions including *'Tis a Pity She's a Whore*, a European tour of *Macbeth*, and the feature films *Baby Boom* and *It Could Happen To You*. His interpretation of Skank as a not-too-bright member of T-Bird's street gang provides some of the film's more humorous moments.

The victim of Eric's first kill, Tin-Tin, is played by Lawrence Mason. He is a first-generation American whose parents are natives of Trinidad. Graduating from New York's High School for the Performing Arts, he made the stage a high priority. His films include *Joey Breaker* and *True Romance*. In order for Mason to portray Tin-Tin, he needed to become very confident with this criminal's weapon of choice.

"Lawrence had no knowledge of knife-fighting," Jeff Imada explained. "I just gave him some lessons, some fundamentals, how to handle a knife, certain fancy twirls and some stances and movements. Since he's supposed to be highly trained, he had to learn some real-life techniques of how a knife-fighter would react to certain things and how he would make them part of himself. When you watch the movie, you'll see that he's very comfortable with the weapons—he's quick with them, he elaborated even more so. I told him to make the motions his own and incorporate how the character would carry them, evolve them into his personal signature."

As Funboy, Michael Masse plays a .44 wielding junkie who lives above The Pit, a grungy bar where T-Bird's gang hangs out. Past roles include that of a transsexual in Monika Treut's 1991 film *My Father Is Coming*. Some of his other film appearances include *Burnesy's Last Call* and *The Cowboy Way*.

Costume Designer Arianne Phillips said that Funboy's outfit was inspired by Iggy Pop, for whom she's designed costumes. Pointing to the tight striped pants that Funboy wears, she confided, "I know Iggy would like these. There is a contemporary quality to his character, but also a seventies sensibility—something of Warhol or D'Allesandro to it. Funboy also wears a happy face T-shirt. This is straight from the comic."

Funboy's druggie girlfriend, Darla is believably portrayed by Anna Thomson. Perhaps best known as the abused prostitute in Clint Eastwood's *Unforgiven*, she has numerous stage, television and film credits including *Fatal Attraction*, *Something Wild*, and *True Romance*.

Her subtle performance makes for one of the more emotional sequences in the film. After being "cleansed" by Eric, Darla gives her all to become a true mother to her neglected daughter, Sarah. A small exchange over breakfast gives a glimmer of hope to the bleak world they inhabit. You may notice it is one of very few scenes with sunlight and without rain.

Also under Top Dollar's rule is sleazy pawnshop owner, Gideon. James O'Barr based the character on a mobster he had seen in the film *Miller's Crossing*; that actor was Jon Polito. Coincidentally, Polito was working on *The Hudsucker Proxy* in the same studio where THE CROW was filming. Polito was able to combine working on both films thus filling O'Barr's ultimate casting choice. Polito began his career on the stage, receiving an Obie award for his performance in *Other People's Money*. Polito was a regular on several TV series including Michael Mann's *Crime Story* and *Homicide: Life on the Street*. He has been in a number of films, including *Barton Fink*, *The Freshman*, *Highlander*, and *The Rocketeer*.

"Gideon's not really a fighter," Jeff Imada explained. "He's just the pawnshop owner. We tried to incorporate how the characters would react, what kind of fighting skills they have or how they would respond in a certain situation, and then accordingly fit in Eric's character, his own style and his reaction to theirs."

When Eric visits him in the pawnshop, it takes Gideon some time to come around and accept that maybe this 'freak' is a little different from his regular clientele. Taken almost directly from the comic book, this scene has Eric digging through a box of rings, each of them representing a life destroyed. He pours the rings into his rifle and takes aim. In a close-up, the rings can be seen shooting out of the barrel just before Gideon's explodes into flames.

Watch for a cameo from creator James O'Barr as a looter carrying a television set. His action distracts Albrecht and allows Eric to escape.

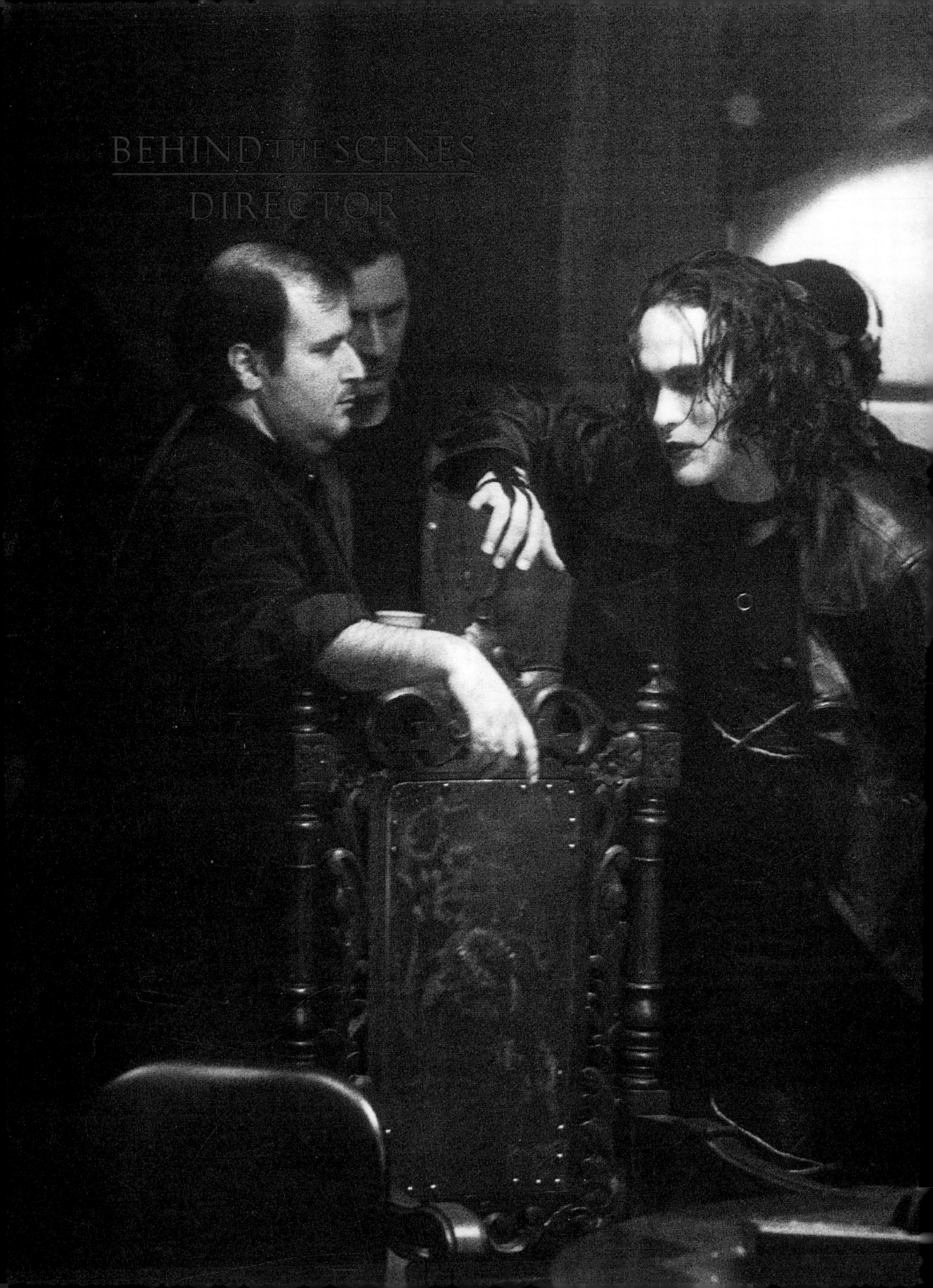
BEHIND THE SCENES
DIRECTOR

AN INTERVIEW WITH ALEX PROYAS

The film is unique. Can you describe the look, your vision for THE CROW?

It *is* different. I guess for me the thing that's appealing is that the hero of the movie has the icons of bad guys in most other movies. He's a sinister looking guy with strange makeup and a very sort of dark presence to him. To make the hero of the movie a character who is back from the dead, that seemed really interesting to me, because usually the villain is something like that in classical drama.

Did you find THE CROW *or did it find you?*

I didn't know anything about it, to be honest. I mean, I'm a big fan of comics, but that's one I'd just never come across before. And you know the first script that was shown to me really was something that, for me, was not what the comic was, and we spent a lot of time really bringing it right back to the flavor of the comic book.

I know that the creator of the comic book, James O'Barr, is very happy, at least with what we're doing on the visual level. For me, the ultimate vision of this film was that it be would shot in black and white because the comic book is black and white and it's a very black and white world that it takes place in. We've tried to give that quality just with the art direction and the lighting. We're being very specific about colors. We're not using any blues or greens. We're only giving it this very dark and expressionist look.

Do you feel the movie is faithful to the comic?

We've tried to be as faithful as we can to the comic book. You know, you're a little torn in this situation, it's not exactly well-known so it's not like everyone seeing this film is going to go, "well, they weren't faithful to the comic book." What appealed to me about the thing was this very evocative mood that's created by the comic book and that's what I wanted to recreate. That's the thing that everyone involved with the film is quite passionate about bringing to the screen. When you look at the comic book you see something in it that really affects you, and it's a very intangible quality, but that's what we're trying to create with the movie as well.

Having something in a visual form like a comic book that you can just look at and go "well that's it"—that's what made me want to make this movie. It's a really great thing. I think that it would be great on any movie to get a comic book made of it first so you can get that locked down and you know what it is that you have. Often with scripts you get to know all the dialogue and stuff in your head and you put the script aside and you start changing things as you go but to have this immediate tool that shows you what it is that you're trying to make is a great thing.

O'Barr said he was very impressed with your use of harsh lighting and fast cuts. Are you using that kind of approach with this film as well?

Yeah, it's a very aggressive style. I want the whole film to feel very confrontational. It's driven by rock and roll music and I want it to feel very energetic and have that raw aggressive quality. I want the images to reflect that.

Can you comment about the use of color in the film?

We had this idea that this film would be very monochromatic, that Eric Draven's life is being drained of all color. It's like he's experiencing this weird dream and we're seeing it with him when he's returned to do his mission. The only real color in the film is during flashbacks, which is kind of a reverse on what usually happens. When you see in memories in films, they're always these sort of drained things, drained of color and life, and they're blurry. I wanted the flashbacks to be the reality, the things that really felt strong, felt more real than what was happening in the rest of the movie.

O'Barr describes the city as a place where angels fear to hover and devils come to preen; and all that is good slinks away and the black night shadows are alive with death.

Hopefully that's what we've put on screen. It's a very empty place. There are very few people in it. You get the feeling that everyone's hiding somewhere. I keep being asked to put more extras into a scene because it feels empty. I have done all these kinds of street shots with one individual walking done the street and no one else to be seen anywhere. That's the quality I'm trying to get, that everyone's almost too scared to come out and it's ended up being bad guys fighting bad guys, and the cops don't know what to do about it and the main character is thrust into that situation.

What is the setting of the film?

Well, it's supposedly set in contemporary Detroit—I'm saying to people that it's like a couple of years in the future. I mean, it's kind of irrelevant. It could be any city in America. I'm trying to take all the real elements from the way the world is but just heighten them a little bit. So, I don't think people seeing the film will necessarily feel it's set in any specific time or place. I wanted it to have this very sort of timeless quality to it.

There is a lot of action in the film. How is it different from other action films?

It has a lot of furious action in it, but it is essentially a romance. I was attracted to the material initially because it was really this very pure story of love and revenge. I think people who like action movies won't be disappointed, but really it's a film about strong passions and people's emotions, and to me that is what is appealing.

Can you talk about the romantic aspect of the film?

Well, it's very important. It's what is driving the character. He's not the Terminator or something; he is a human being pushed into these remarkable situations. He has fairly unique gifts but he still reacts to them in a very human way. To me, it is as romantic as it can be within the confines of the fantasy.

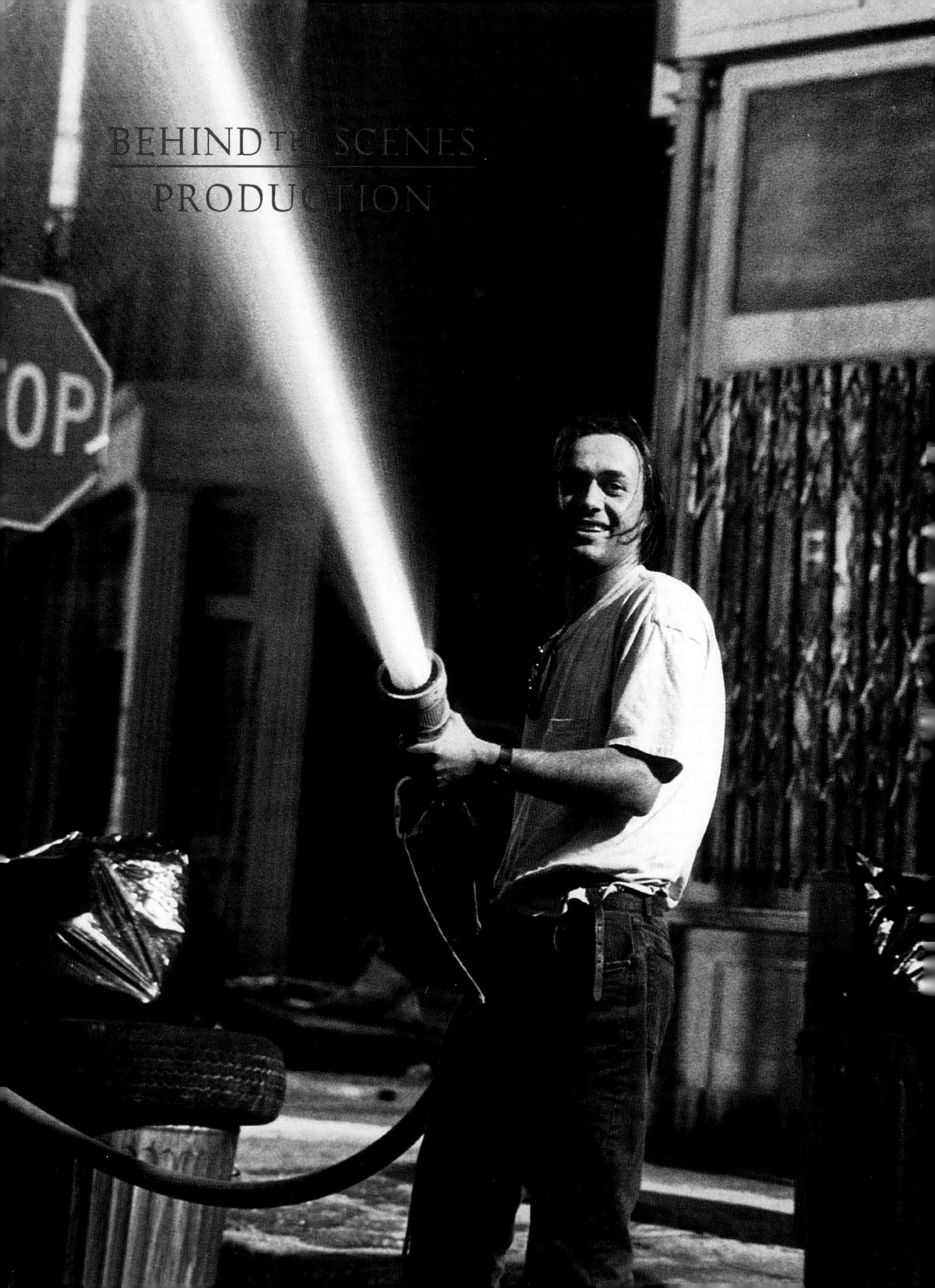

Back in the early stages of pre-production, the original plan was to film THE CROW on location in Los Angeles. However, director Alex Proyas was adamant about wanting the control that soundstages provide, so ultimately the production was based at the Carolco Studios in Wilmington, North Carolina, an independent facility complete with sound-stages and a backlot featuring a New York City street. Started in the mid-seventies by producer Dino De Laurentiis, the studio is now a bustling center for a variety of non-studio, foreign and television productions.

ALEX McDOWELL - PRODUCTION DESIGNER

"As far as I was concerned, the comic book was the biggest factor in the look. I think people who know the comic will absolutely recognize it in the film. Eric is a very believable, strong, avenging character. I think that everything that was powerful about that character in the comic comes through. For our purposes his motivations were always the underlying influence on the look."

Alex McDowell's career began in London in the late '70s, designing album covers for bands like The Cure and Siouxsie and the Banshees. Later he worked as an art director on music videos and even directed a few himself. "Alex Proyas met a lot of other designers," said McDowell. A few of these designers had some hefty resumes, whereas McDowell was young and his biggest film to date was *The Lawnmower Man*. But Proyas wanted to use him and anyone who sees the film can immediately discern how astute a decision that was.

"I think that the starting point for the design was, obviously, the comic book," McDowell said. "The imagery of that is great, and it is also very simple. I liked it a lot. We tried to take the simplicity of the comic book to the film. The setting is a decayed inner city; a place that has gone so far down the tubes it's beyond redemption. We really wanted to get across that the city is a like a war zone."

McDowell flew to Michigan during the first few weeks of pre-production. He was taken around the city by a man from the chamber of commerce. This lovely scenic tour showed off such attractions as the new civic center. Sensing that perhaps he wasn't seeing the city represented by the comic, Alex called James O'Barr and, never having met him, arrived at his house. Alex remembers the creator as being very quiet and withdrawn. "I was just very interested and I had a chance to pick his brain and really go into it," said McDowell. "He took me around the streets of Detroit and he would point to an empty lot and say 'this is where the bar The Pit was based on used to be,' and at some rubble, 'this is where I lived.' It was just amazing that only ten years later there was nothing left."

Exteriors and master shots were to be taken of actual locations in Detroit, but once McDowell actually saw the city he realized there was no way this could be done. On so many blocks there would be just one building still up surrounded by utter devastation. O'Barr contends that fires are set by locals; if a building was empty they would burn it down to prevent its transformation into a crack house.

And though the point was never to recreate Detroit, McDowell did try to incorporate some of its particular attributes. "I got a really strong sense of elevated motorways, freeways in that area where O'Barr originally lived," he said. "There is some bridge going to Canada or something. There's this sense that you're down here and there is all this stuff up there. And we definitely tried to do that in the original drawings. We wanted the church to have the feeling of being under this freeway. But it was purely a cost thing, we couldn't build that structure."

Obviously, there were influences on the design of the film other than Detroit and some of these, aptly enough, had been influences on O'Barr. "We wanted to get the comic book across drawing on German Expressionist films like *The Cabinet of Doctor Caligari* and *Pandora's Box*," McDowell recalled. "Once I talked to O'Barr, I discovered that those were also some of his influences. Very black, very angular, very dark."

"The look of the film came from a concept to see the events through the eyes of the central

Top: The city as visualized by Alex McDowell with illustration by Darren Gilford. Bottom: THE CROW backlot.

Clockwise top left to right: Gideon's set design by
Alex McDowell, illustrations by Darren Gilford;
Gideon's pawnshop recreated on location in
North Carolina; Brandon Lee in loft; storyboard
artist Peter Pound's visualization of loft.

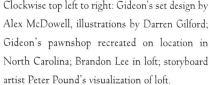

character," Proyas stated. "I felt that we should be looking at a real world, not a Hollywood fabrication, but stylized in the sense that our character is seeing it stripped of life, devoid of color. His true life is the one that was taken from him. We only ever see it as a flashback—thus the vibrant use of color in these sequences; it hurts for him to remember."

"The gloom of the film is very important, no sunlight essentially," echoed McDowell. "Right from the first meeting we discussed eliminating greens and blues and controlling the palette completely. We really tried to create a monochromatic palette, but with red. The idea is that Eric's vision, when he comes back from the grave, is totally bleak. He's got nothing to look forward to at all. And the addition of red I saw as the color of revenge. I thought it was used that way in the film and in the comic."

The undeniable musical influence of O'Barr's story also needed to be prevalent in the film. "The nightclub is important because we could use it to really hammer home the idea that the music has a lot to do with the characters," said McDowell. "We drew upon the kind of end of the world sensibility that punk had about it. Club Trash is based on a combination of clubs that I have been to in the last ten years. We had all been to that special kind of illegal underground night-

club, what would now be called a rave, where people just take over existing premises without doing anything to them. We had been in luck that at this location there is a great, deserted concrete factory; it's used for filming but it is what every nightclub owner would be looking for. The idea is that Top Dollar lives above the nightclub and we were actually able to do that with this space. We literally set his office four floors up and he can look down."

McDowell made the cathedral his central design point. "The church is a great basis for the gothic look of the whole film, and we brought elements into Eric's home. Alex wanted a round window and the loft supports evolved naturally. The loft was like a nest at the top of this building."

"The use of miniatures grew out of a fairly practical consideration. I had this idea of being with the crow flying through the city at night way up in the air. The only way to do it was to do it in miniature and mat the crow into the scene. Out of those images really came the whole style of the film."

—Director Alex Proyas

The miniatures were built by Gus Ramsden who lives in Wilmington, North Carolina, and who actually built almost everything himself with one assistant. Ramsden can simply look at a picture and then be able to make a model of it. He drew upon disparate elements to create the buildings: Alex McDowell's pictures of the Detroit skyline, storyboard artist Peter Pound's sketches, and also Eugene Atget's photography from the 1900s. "He was a major influence on the Surrealists," McDowell said of the latter, "because he photographed all these empty streets and empty graveyards, just completely deserted."

When McDowell and Ramsden first began working, they didn't know what buildings would be needed. "Gus started developing parts, just brick and stone, sheets of surface, because early on we had no idea of the kind of geography we'd need for the city," Remembered Alex. "He was producing the raw elements that could be used as a city and had the right look to them. We got ten or fifteen buildings started which were just the right look and could be used in a lot of different situations. All miniatures. Then, as we started developing the street on the backlot, we got specific about the hotel building, The Pit and Gideon's, and the architecture of the ground because we were tied into that backlot. [They had to make it correspond to the place where they were shooting outside.] What we called Eric's entrance was an actual three- or four-story building that had store-fronts [where Sarah goes and pulls off the boards]. But we also had a miniature that matched, and so we could link Eric's apartment to the front of the building. In the end, a lot of the process was just chopping a building up, cutting it in half or putting a different top on it."

It was originally thought that the climactic rooftop scene, the duel between Top Dollar and Eric, might be shot on actual roofs. But they did some location scouting and were unable to find any appropriately gothic roofs in Wilmington's vicinity. So Ramsden constructed modular full-scale rooftops and these were connected, filling one entire stage. "The actual scale of the cathedral miniature was 12th scale," McDowell pointed out. "It was really big. The spires were eight or ten feet tall."

Dariusz Wolski would light the miniatures and Andrew Mason, the second unit director and Proyas's associate of many years, would direct. But shooting the miniatures was pushed back. Gus Ramsden then had to transport the miniatures from Wilmington to Simi Valley, a suburb just northeast of Los Angeles. "It was crazy in a way because the whole set was built in resin which was unusual; it was cheaper to make them that way but they were very fragile," McDowell said. "But they survived the trip, and they carried on building at Dream Quest. The first time the city was actually put together in one place was at Dream Quest. Then it was like 'we need more of this, we need more of that.' Gus did a remarkable job."

DARIUSZ WOLSKI - DIRECTOR OF PHOTOGRAPHY

Dariusz "Derek" Wolski came onto the picture very early in the process. He had worked with Alex Proyas on many music videos and commercials. The two of them had spent so much time working together that they had a sort of aesthetic shorthand. It was no problem communicating, but their ideas were so grand that logistically shooting the film proved to be a huge undertaking.

"The amazing thing with me and Alex is that he's from Australia and I'm from Poland but we have these similar heroes and loves," the cinematographer stated. "THE CROW is action-oriented, but the sensitivity, shooting everything very moody, dark and mysterious; it was like we were absolutely insane. But for me it was a blessing to have a director like this. The rest of the industry is very much 'we want to see this, we want to see that.' So to work together and create what we wanted, it was like a dream."

There were often three cameras shooting during a scene, sometimes as many as ten, with the cameras all running at different speeds. "You learn you have to approach things differently," Wolski explained "With Alex it's just fantastic because he knows that he needs that camera there for a shot that just lasts three seconds. With multi-camera setups, you have to learn to deal with the whole space. You can't just light one picture where you shoot someone and then shoot the reverse angle. Instead you have to design the whole thing, you have to know how it will work. And, of course, the seventh camera comes in at such an impossible place, you just have to trust the director and believe that this is going to work perfectly.

"Alex is a man who loves challenges. He would tell us, all the technical people, what he wanted and we would try to figure out how to do it. This was my first film of this caliber, but

I wasn't afraid because with Alex, he knows just how to get as much out of you as he possibly can. He understands that we are all taking chances and pushing everything very far. If something doesn't work, he will find a solution and it can be really quite amazing. Ed Pressman is a great producer and he gave us a lot of freedom. It's an ideal situation for a cameraman to work in. If this had been a normal big studio film there would have been a lot of cooks all giving their opinion."

Dariusz also made the trip to Dream Quest. "I was involved in shooting the miniatures," said Wolski. "I learned a lot. It's one of those things they tell you, 'Oh no, you don't have to come, we have a miniature cameraman, and you say 'okay, that's fine.' But the people doing it are young and not so experienced. Basically, they needed to do the same things that we had done while shooting live action except scaled down. They couldn't quite grasp it in the beginning, but later they were completely into it. Miniature shooting is time-consuming, so for me the lighting might take five hours but in order to use those five hours I have to be there for four or five days. It's kind of insane. Once they learned what I was after they did everything and I was just coming in to tweak things."

The manner in which live action and miniature are integrated in the finished film is unique and definitely a big part of the stunning impact of THE CROW. It seems especially remarkable in the car chase sequences. These scenes have a beauty all their own. "It was hard, it was very hard," remarked Wolski. "Every time we had a car chase everyone said, 'How is that going to work?' but Alex's approach is not to be afraid of anything. He made it work."

ARIANNE PHILLIPS ON COSTUME DESIGN

"I came onto THE CROW in kind of an unusual way. I knew Brandon because of some print work and promotion he did before this. He knew that I had been working in rock and roll for a long time. He took me aside and said that he had thought about me and that I would be good for this movie, that it was about this rock and roll singer who comes back from the dead. At first I didn't take it seriously, but he showed me the comic book and I said, 'This is really, really great!' When Brandon told me who was working on the project: Alex McDowell, Alex Proyas and Derek Wolski, I knew I had to be on this project. Whatever it took!

"I went into the interview and Alex and I immediately hit it off. We started talking and one of the things I asked about was the references to music; there was a quote from Joy Division and there was a little picture of Ian Curtis. I grew up in the '70s and the early '80s was a pivotal time for me. I had just left high school and Joy Division, The Cure, Bauhaus and Peter Murphy were what I listened to. This was one of the things I could give to the movie, an understanding of that music.

"In the movie, the line between fantasy and reality is breached and you can play with it. In the comic there is also a great poignancy, a deep emotional level that has been transferred to the film. The acting is really great. It's wonderful to be able to see a comic book come to life in a film without being 'comic booky'; there is a reality to it. What I could do was give it some grittiness as well as panache and excitement.

"Eric Draven's costume is lifted directly from the comic; it was never questioned. It's really a wonderful piece with a lot of flavor to it. Eric steals it from Tin-Tin, one of the bad guys. We felt Eric should also be wearing leather pants, so there would be a weightiness to them, some substance.

"There is a color design to the whole film that I went along with. It's wonderful to work with Alex Proyas; he is very specific about what he wants colorwise and about the silhouettes of the characters and the textures. There is not a lot of color in the film. It's monochromatic with black, brown and grey. There is also a certain amount of red, especially in the female characters. Myca wears this red headpiece I worked on with designer Rick Owens. It's almost a kind of bondage piece; it laces in the back. You know she's evil, so she was fun. She is a woman who is a kind of beautiful siren. She has psychic powers so she had to have a very strong presence."

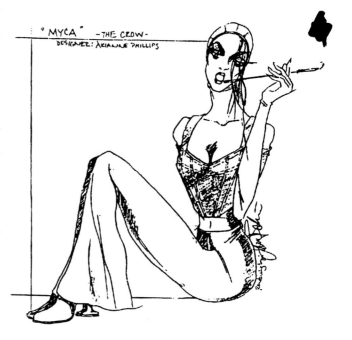

"MYCA" —THE CROW—
DESIGNER: ARIANNE PHILLIPS

SPECIAL EFFECTS
AN INTERVIEW WITH
LANCE ANDERSON

How much time did you have to prepare?

For this film, I had pre-production of about eight weeks. We made the birds, arms and legs in my lab in Los Angeles before leaving. The burnt corpse of T-Bird I happened to have, I just doctored it up and they took photographs for the police stills. We got there [Wilmington] in December and we set up a lab there.

Brandon was a real sweetheart to work with; he had to be so patient. I took shots of him during pre-production so that I could make full body casts. I also had to make body parts, of hands and chests, because I had to do a lot of scars, where he takes bullet hits. We did [Michael] Wincott's head and Bai Ling's face right away. They'd have to hold [an expression] for about thirty minutes. Then we'd clean it up and make it as good as we could to make molds.

How were Brandon's hand slits done?

We had mechanical hands that matched the actor and they closed up on cue. What we ended up doing was closing it to a point and then going in there and shooting a few frames and then taking filler and filling the hole in so it would close totally clean and go away, like stop-motion.

Did you also do Brandon's actual performance makeup?

Yeah, I did that also. Usually it took about thirty-five minutes to apply, but it was closer to an hour in the beginning. I had a rubber mask that had the slices in it. That helped me lay down the pattern so that it would always be the same: the vertical lines around the eyes and the corners of the mouth. He also had a scar across the top of the nose. So for all of these I made reference marks, a kind of rubber template.

The scene where Eric intervenes with Darla is very effective. How was the effect on Darla's arm done?

My assistant Steve Coulter and I had a fake arm and an appliance on her. On the fake arm we pulled stuff through to make it look like the veins were rippling and then we had a closer shot of her with the drip and they ended up using that primarily, but the rippling effect looked great.

What about Bai Ling's tattoos?

The tattoos were designed and applied by a local tattoo artist who actually came on the set and did them. He made a template and then he hand-painted it in.

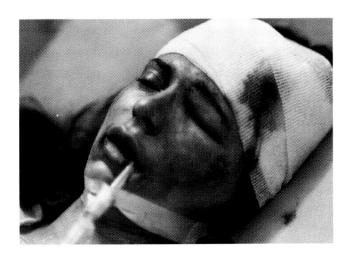

The scenes of Shelly in the hospital are hard to take. Even Sofia Shinas said she couldn't bear to look at herself.

We had an appliance for the swollen cheek. The whole thing took about two hours to apply. I have a lot of books on forensic pathology. It's embedded in my mind now.

Would you talk a little about Top Dollar's death?

We did a life cast of him. I took a lot of reference photos so I could compare the color and help with the sculpting. The dummy was on a counterbalanced slide mechanism, so the body was suspended out in the air and would then plunge down. We also had a blood gag rigged in the gargoyle's mouth so it would start gushing blood.

We had tubes coming up through the body and out through the mouth so when the horn came out of the mouth it would spurt.

There were also blood tubes all around in his chest. There were two of us that had these pumps, like giant syringes. So we measured it and as soon as the body got to this certain point we'd push down on these huge syringes, one on either side, and it just gushed out.

They had two or three cameras on it. It was going to be a dummy going down, and when they pulled back the camera it would be him. We had a fake thing that he held in his mouth and a fake horn sticking out of his chest.

You mentioned that you made mechanical birds?

Yes, but the real birds could do a lot of things. The birds were amazing, they worked so well. I had them in my studio to study them and make reference material so I could create the mechanical birds for when we needed them. We had to use them in the scene with Bai Ling; initially the bird with her is the real bird but then when it really attacks her we had to use the mechanical bird. There were separate wing controls and separate claw controls. I was operating the claws.

The crows were actually ravens. The set designer Alex McDowell, mentioned how incredible the birds were on the set. "The crows were amazing," McDowell remembers them training in the backlot. " Just to see them. They would practice every night with the rain machines. The crow would come out of the rain straight to its trainer."

AN INTERVIEW WITH LARRY MADRID-ANIMAL TRAINER

Let's talk about your collaborative efforts with the ravens to make THE CROW *what it is.*

Actually it's a technique that I learned from the company I work for, Birds and Animals Unlimited. The owner has been an animal trainer for over thirty years. He goes as far back as Alfred Hitchcock's *The Birds*. He developed a lot and passed down that knowledge and put it to work.

You get the ravens as babies and hand raise them. They learn to associate you with companionship and a food source. As they mature, you take them through the whole process of learning how to fly to you and take direction. They are actually really intelligent. They can be taught to do a variety of things.

This picture was all scheduled to shoot at night, the time the ravens usually sleep. It was supposed to take place in the rain which is not a natural thing for them. So it was just really challenging. We had to train them toward evening after the sun had gone down. Also, it just happened that we got a lot of rain, which was good.

What kind of stunts were the crows doing?

You have your basic A to B, flying from one place to another. Then you have flying to me. We had to train the raven to sit on Brandon's shoulder and be comfortable sitting there. We really spent a lot of time teaching him to sit on someone's shoulder and not get aggressive toward their face. The beak could do a lot of damage to someone. We had a pre-production meeting with Jeff Imada, the director, 1st AD, the producer, and Brandon. I told them about my concerns and the precautions we would take and Brandon was very cool about it. He was totally relaxed and the training with Brandon went really well. He really liked animals a lot and he took it all lightheartedly. He even made jokes about how it would be okay if later on he would have to wear a patch, because he's always wanted to do a pirate film. When the time came to transfer some of the bond that I had with the birds to Brandon he had already spent a lot of time feeding them. The birds would fly to him in just about any situation and comfortably sit on his shoulder without posing any danger to him whatsoever. I felt totally confident having the ravens on him.

Did you have a training regimen?

I train seven days a week and I trained five ravens, two of them I had personally raised. There was another trainer also, as we needed two on this job. What I did was break down the script. The things I needed to concentrate on were the rain, working at night, and turning the bird's schedule around. I would keep track of what each raven did best. One would fly better or one may be intimidated by the camera boom. However Magic and Omen, the two ravens we used most, were interchangeable. I had raised and trained Magic. He was the lead raven.

What about the shots where the camera is tracking alongside the raven against a blue screen?

What I did was train the ravens to fly in a wind machine. We put a baffle in front and angled it in such a manner that the raven would go up and hover until I asked them to come down and rewarded them for their good behavior.

Do they respond to verbal commands?

We use both verbal and hand cues, so I work with

them a lot like a dog, and you can relate to them in that way.

There is an amazing shot where Brandon breaks through a glass door and barely a second later the crow follows him and goes right up to the camera. How did you manage that?

It's based on trust and bonding with them. We trained without the glass there so the raven did it enough times he thought, "Oh, this is what I am supposed to do. I fly through and go over there and land." It seemed cool, and we get ready to do it, and Brandon goes through the glass and for all practical purposes it looks the same except there might be some glass falling. The raven had to deal with that but basically, he had already committed himself at that point. It was his trust in me that made him go ahead and come to me anyway. It was a very challenging shot, but honestly, he only did it that one time. He wouldn't do a second take because he learned. He was too smart to do it again.

THE MUSIC

"It was very important to me that we use rock and roll in the film. There have been a lot of movies made and you don't hear any of it in the film because its always underplayed. It's done as a promotional tool so that they can release an album. I like rock and roll and I wanted to use it upfront to drive the story and the whole pace of the film. We constructed it almost as a series of musical numbers. A lot were chosen very early on in the process and often the writing was done having a particular song in mind. I just found that it gave the whole thing a very operatic feeling for the larger than life passions that were involved. It does certainly make the thing feel very energetic."

—Director Alex Proyas

Described in an early review as the soundtrack album of the century, THE CROW soundtrack is a true reflection of the touchstones that inspired both the original comic and the film itself. The cutting edge music for THE CROW is central to the vision of the film's creators.

"At one point, I was asked who I'd like to see on the soundtrack," said THE CROW creator James O'Barr. "I sent producer Jeff Most a short list of my favorite artists and didn't think anything would come of it. Amazingly, they were able to get seventy-five percent of them."

The music is the fitting accompaniment to the dark world of love and revenge depicted in the comic and brought to the screen. The bands contributing are: The Cure; Machines of Loving Grace; Stone Temple Pilots; Nine Inch Nails; Rage Against the Machine; Violent Femmes; Rollins Band; Helmet; Pantera; For Love Not Lisa; My Life with the Thrill Kill Kult; The Jesus and Mary Chain; Medicine; and Jane Siberry.

THE SCORE-
AN INTERVIEW WITH
GRAEME REVELL

Graeme Revell was born in New Zealand. His musical education consists of classical training on piano and French horn. He graduated from the University of Auckland in 1974 with degrees in politics and economics, and from there went to Paris to study philosophy.

In 1978, while working as a psychiatric nurse in Sydney, Australia, Revell formed the avante-garde experimental group, SPK (Surgical Penis Klinic). The band was based in London from 1980 to 1985 where they made their major label debut with Elektra Records. When the album failed to live up to critical expectations, Graeme disbanded the group. He went on to record an obscure (but well-reviewed) solo album before returning to Australia.

It was by sheer happenstance that he was able to score the Australian suspense thriller *Dead Calm*, which has since taken him all over the world, scoring such films as John Woo's *Hard Target*, and Wim Wenders's *Until the End of the World*, as well as the thrillers *The Hand That Rocks the Cradle*, *The Crush*, *Child's Play 2* and *No Escape*.

What was your influence for the incidental music in THE CROW?

The songs. I'm happy to admit that I think the young audience really does focus more on the songs than on the score. But I think that subliminally, the score is actually what delivers the impact of the movie, particularly in this case where the emotional center has to shift focus from Eric to Sarah.

"It Can't Rain All The Time" seems to be the theme for the spirit of the film. Had you worked with Jane Siberry before on Until the End of the World?

No. She happens to be on it, and I love that track. It was a wonderful experience to work with her on this. She had never collaborated with anyone before. Her agent said, "Forget it, don't even bother talking to her." But I did and said, "Look, I think you'll really be surprised, you should see this movie." She is definitely the kind of person who is not inclined to outright violent displays; there has to be some kind of reasoning or some moral behind it. When she saw it she said she found it one of the most affecting films she's seen for a long time.

The movie has a kind of displaced sense of time. Was that a factor in the score?

It sort of speaks to me of the future a little bit. I think of a kind of multi-ethnic thing even though the film didn't really show it and it's supposed to be Detroit (laughs). To be specific, the music is really Turkish Armenian. I got Gasparian, the greatest duduk player in the world, at great cost and

it was worth it. But Alex thought the music was too Arabic so I would shadow it with vocals and both things sounded like something else. I thought it really worked.

Alex said he wanted to make the rock and roll songs integral to specific scenes. Do you feel that your music was then downplayed?

Yeah, for example, the sort of Arabic theme that opens the film is not heard because of the voice-over. Things like that happen and I don't really mind. I'm not one of those composers who fights, nail and tooth over every little note. I'm usually just happy to see the movie work.

ON THE CUTTING ROOM FLOOR

Virtually every major film experiences mid-course corrections and post-production adjustments. It's not uncommon for entire scenes to be dropped due to time or budgetary constraints, and later on additional scenes might also be deemed unnecessary and removed. Sometimes other elements just do not work on the screen as planned.

Early in the film, we see T-Bird and his gang torch Arcade Games. As originally filmed, a woman named Alison is victimized and left to die in the ensuing firebomb. But Eric, following the crow, arrives at the building just after it explodes. With the woman fading fast in his arms, Eric gets the first of the many "memory flashes," painful psychic bursts brought on by contact with people. He sees Tin-Tin and T-Bird menacing their most recent victim, Alison. These searing bits of total recall provide Eric with clues about what happened to him and Shelly—but it also gives us a brief preview of Eric's powers and of things to come.

T-Bird and Skank set out on another arson run. "Smokes and road beers," orders T-Bird to his mushmouthed flunky. "I'm on it," Skank, the speedfreak replies. As originally constructed, Skank is loading up on supplies when two pre-teens enter the store, pull out automatic weapons and appropriate his .45.

Outside, Eric gets the drop on T-Bird in his muscle car and forces the gang leader to drive off. Skank sees the hijacking and instinctively gives chase, forgetting the gun-toting robbers. He escapes from the store only to be shot in the leg by one of the young hoodlums with his own gun. Skank painfully hobbles out into the street where he's hit by the square John in the Japanese sub-compact. "What a classic," the kids yell, laughing hysterically at Skank's antics.

"The original idea for this scene," explained screenwriter David J. Schow, "was to show how utterly random the violence was in that city; that it could occur to anyone at any time, even the bad guys. In fact, I wanted Eric and Shelly's deaths to be a random incident as well: the gang went to the wrong apartment, it was all a mistake. To me this is closer to the comic, where Eric and Shelly are killed by street thugs on a joy ride."

The scene was trimmed of its youthful offenders, and now only sharp-eyed viewers will notice Skank stiff-legging his way out of the liquor store (after he's hit by the car, it's easy to imagine why he's limping). But no amount of study will spot Top Dollar's body tattoos. Like his half-sister Myca, Top Dollar also sported some impressive tribalistic body art, but, due to time considerations, these scenes were not filmed.

Early versions of the script contained an Asian menace out to steal Eric's powers for his own evil pursuits. At Brandon Lee's behest, the super-villain character was dropped altogether. The role of Top Dollar was then elevated and expanded, and his half-sister/lover, Myca, invented in order to retain some of the toned-down mystical elements.

Also revamped was the Skull Cowboy. In O'Barr's graphic novel, a grinning skeletal spirit is seen only three times—a metaphoric manifestation of Eric's anguished mental state. Schow first extrapolated this image into a minor character, an earthbound spirit guide in a rotting duster who tells the newly resurrected Eric to "follow the crow." Later, after Eric has strayed from his mission of retribution, the Skull Cowboy reappears, saying: "I told you to follow the bird."

This crumbling cowpoke character evolved throughout script rewrites into an ethereal mentor, clearly spelling out to Eric the terms of his temporary resurrection: ice the bad guys, receive a reunion with Shelly—but "work for the living, you bleed." This element of ultimate doom put Eric's afterlife in jeopardy, adding to the suspense and drama.

"I decided to cut the Skull Cowboy for a variety of reasons," said director Alex Proyas, "but chiefly because the scenes became somewhat redundant. It is true, however, that I wasn't happy with the effect—the technique used to create the cowboy. By this I don't mean to diminish Michael Berryman's work in any way—I felt I hadn't given him the visual support he needed to bring this character to life convincingly."

Special makeup effects master Lance Anderson was in charge of creating the elaborate live-action creature. "There was going to be this whole thing where Eric was with

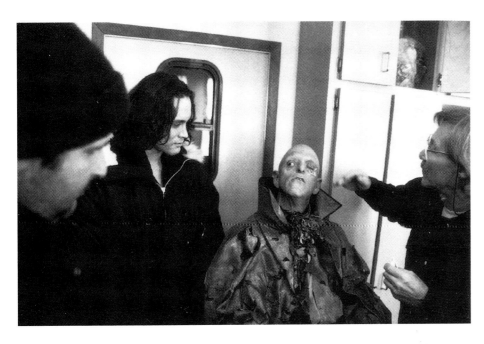

the Skull Cowboy when he disintegrated," explained Anderson.

This was to have taken place on the church steps just prior to the final confrontation between Eric and Top Dollar. The Skull Cowboy warns Eric that, having just killed Skank in the shoot-out at Club Trash, his mission is over, and he must return to the grave and forget the concerns of the living. Eric knows that Sarah has been kidnapped by Top Dollar, and that acting in the affairs of the material world will likely prevent his reunion with Shelly. Eric proceeds, refusing to abandon his young friend. "Then choose and be damned," intones the Skull Cowboy, as a whirlwind rises up around them. The skeletal figure crumbles away into coffin dust as Eric bulls his way up the church steps, knowing that he'll face Top Dollar's attack as a mortal.

"It was all going to be done in post-production, a computer thing. We were going to take elements of the Skull Cowboy, parts of the body, and they were going to fly around Eric in a circle, like in a vortex, as he disintegrated." Said Anderson of the cut, "I think they were trying to make more of a compassionate personal relationship story out of it, less supernatural. Michael Berryman was really disappointed when his scenes were lost." (He had recommended Berryman for the job originally, having worked with him on *My Science Project*.)

Potential fan disappointment aside, the Skull Cowboy did seem to detract more than add to the picture; and by having only one supernatural character, the film's narrative is more focused and cohesive. But because this character was no longer in the film, the storyline's continuity was in jeopardy. There was the concept of Eric's restorative powers diminishing whenever he works for the living. Now a completely staged scene had to be removed; a second fight between Funboy and Eric.

Eric shoots Funboy in the leg and drags the unconscious druggie into the bathroom where Darla cowers, armed with a straight razor. Eric dumps him in the shower and then confronts Darla, whereupon he uses his healing powers to expel morphine from her veins. After Darla runs out of the apartment, we see Eric examining one of Funboy's syringes just as the scene cuts away. What we don't see is a berserk Funboy's sneak attack, wielding the straight razor Darla dropped on the bathroom floor.

Stunt coordinator Jeff Imada described the sequence: "The fight begins at the door when Eric picks up the hypo. Funboy slashes him across the back, driving him down on his knees. Eric is stunned, in shock, showing a lot of pain; Funboy grabs a big bag of coke

"The thing about this scene," Imada stated, "is that Eric is in pain the whole time, really hurt. His fighting is totally defensive, he's just trying to find an open area and keep himself going. It was a very non-technical fight, very real. It's only out of desperation that he's finally able to regain himself. It let the audience see a different part of Eric."

This razor fight was to motivate Eric to use black electrical tape as a homemade bandage. This fashion accessory comes directly from the comic and helps define his look. James O'Barr had Eric carve up his own arms with a razor during a particularly nasty episode of despair—the wounds are self-inflicted, which is why they don't heal and must be taped. Now the black bandages seem to appear in the film for no reason, but they look great!

and just inhales it, just going for it." Surprisingly, Eric's wounds aren't healing, a result of his benign interaction with Darla; working for the living.

Imada continued: "Funboy—now totally jacked up, coke all over his face—jumps on Eric and starts slashing him some more. Eric rolls over on his back, fending off Funboy's attack with his arms, which are getting all cut up. Funboy tries to slash Eric's face and neck, but Eric knocks him away and they struggle on the floor. Eric finally knocks Funboy back against some furniture, tables and lamps and stuff, and the straight razor goes flying. He goes after his gun, which Eric had left on his bed. This gives Eric a little bit of advantage, he does this throw, and knocks Funboy down to the ground, groggy. Then Eric reaches for the hypo again.

Though not highly publicized, the results of Dream Quest's

efforts are truly remarkable; a seamless blending of elements that extends the reality of scenes in a way that could not have been possible when the picture was actually in production.

THE CROW was shooting in the loft set when the tragic accident took Brandon Lee's life. There were some eight days of shooting left, mostly centered on this location, and mostly concerned with Eric and Shelly's life together, but also encompassing Eric's post-murder activities there, such as reliving moments of his death, putting on the whiteface makeup, burning the pictures of Shelly, and meeting with Sarah.

Though the bulk of the footage for these sequences employed a live double (usually shown in shadow), Dream Quest Images' digital compositing unit broke new ground in their contribution to help complete seven scenes by adapting footage of Brandon from other sequences. Two examples of their work are the shots of Eric entering the abandoned loft, and his reflection in the broken mirror.

For the latter effect, an image of a rain-soaked Eric was digitally isolated (a computer version of the old roto-scoping technique, where a hold-out matte is created, or finished, by hand, much like traditional cel painting for animation) and then composited into a view of the shattered mirror. To help with the task, a reference shot was taken with a stand-in so that a displacement map could be created. By reformatting Eric's image using this displacement grid, and then compositing the resulting image with the shot of the mirror, a remarkable replication of an anguished, "fractured" Eric was accomplished.

For the view of Eric entering his loft, another alley scene was used, again with the background, and rain, digitally erased. Now, instead of stumbling down the alley, Eric appears to be lurching through the doorway of his old apartment (a simple matte of the doorway completed the illusion).

While digital mattes and computer compositing have been around for a few years now, the techniques have usually been employed "traditionally," namely for putting actors into matte paintings and other so-called "plate" imagery, or for wire removal and clean-up of stunt shots. Needless to say, these special effects shots are planned well in advance, which usually means having a steady, locked-off camera shoot the various "plate" elements, or, as is now common, a computer-controlled motion-control rig (which can replay the exact camera moves, thus insuring that the different elements will line up when composited together).

But the elements used on THE CROW had been filmed without any regard to special post-production optical work; so, no motion-control camera, no locked-off photography. In fact, Dream Quest had to make do with mostly hand-held footage, which had constant movement on all axes. It was only by dint of experimental image-tracking software being developed at the time that this "wild" footage could be successfully transplanted into other scenes, and thus put the subtle finishing touches on the film.

Miramax/Dimension Films
Presents

An
Edward R. Pressman Production

In Association With
Jeff Most Productions

"THE CROW"

Music Score Composed by
Graeme Revell

Production Designer
Alex McDowell

Edited By
Dov Hoenig, A.C.E.
and Scott Smith

Director of Photography
Dariusz Wolski

Co-Producers
Caldecot Chubb
and James A. Janowitz

Executive Producer
Robert L. Rosen

Based on the comic book series
and comic strip by James O'Barr

Screenplay by
David J. Schow
and John Shirley

Produced by
Edward R. Pressman
and Jeff Most

Directed by
Alex Proyas

Soundtrack Available on
Atlantic Records-Interscope
Records, Cassettes
and Compact Discs

Eric Brandon Lee
Albrecht Ernie Hudson
Top Dollar Michael Wincott
T-Bird David Patrick Kelly
Skank Angel David
Sarah Rochelle Davis
Myca Bai Ling
Tin Tin Lawrence Mason
Funboy Michael Massee
Mickey Bill Raymond
Torres Marco Rodriguez
Shelly Sofia Shinas
Darla Anna Thomson
Grange Tony Todd
Gideon Jon Polito
Annabella Kim Sykes
Lead Cop Rock Taulbee
Roscoe Norman "Max" Maxwell
Waldo Jeff Cadiente
MJ Henry Kingi, Jr.
Speeg Erik Stabenau
Newscaster Cassandra Lawton
Uniform Cop #1 Lou Criscuolo
Paramedic #1 Todd Brenner
Paramedic #2 Joe West
Sanchez Tom Rosales
Braeden Jeff Imada
Jugger Tierre Turner
Bad Ass Criminal Tim Parati

Medicine
James Goodall Brad Laner
James Putnam Eddie Ruscha
Elizabeth Thompson

My Life with The Thrill Kill Kult
Marston Daley Laura Gomel
Rachel Hollingsworth Charles Levi
Mark McCabe Frank Nardiello

Stunt Coordinator Jeff Imad[a]

Fight Choreograph[er]
Brandon Lee and Jeff Imad[a]

Stunt Performer[s]
Jeff Cadient[e]
Rick Avery Buddy Joe Hooke[r]
Bobby Bass Brian Imad[a]
Ken Bates Matt Johnsto[n]
Sandy Berumen Dean Mumfor[d]
Simone Boiseree Alan Oline[r]
Troy Brown Eric Ronde[l]
Bob Brown Ronnie Ronde[l]
Steve Chambers Gilbert Rosale[s]
John Copeman Lori Lynn Ros[s]
Chris Durand Chad Stahelsk[i]
Dale Frye John Stonham, S[r.]
Al Goto John Stonham, J[r.]
Ric Waug[h]

Art Director Simon Murt[on]
Costume Designer Arianne Philli[ps]
Casting Directors Billy Hopki[ns]
Suzanne Smi[th]
Associate Producer Gregory A. Ga[le]
Associate Producer/Production Manag[er]
Grant H[ill]
1st Assistant Director Steve Andre[ws]
2nd Assistant Director Randall LaFolle[tt]
Unit Production Manager (Added Scenes) [Bob]
Rond[ell]
Music Supervisor Jolene Che[rry]
Visual Effects Supervisor/2nd Unit Director Andre[w]
Mas[on]
Assistant Art Director Geoffrey S. Grimsm[an]
Set Decorator Marthe Pine[au]
Storyboard Artists Peter Pou[nd]
Hannah Stra[ub]
Set Designer William Barc[lay]
Leadman John Kretschm[er]
Assistant Art Department Coordinator Jeff Tanr[er]
Camera Operators David Cr[one]
Ken Arli[ck]
1st Assistant Camera John Vera[rt]
John Cambria Fredrick "Chip" Hack[er]
2nd Assistant Camera George He[rst]
Michael Satraze[n]
Camera Loaders Ken Huds[on]
Mary Lou Vet[o]
Video Assistants Charles Laugh[lin]
Mark McMa[hon]
Still Photographer Robert Zuckerm[an]

Sound Mixer **Buddy Alper**

Boom Operator **Byron Eugene Ashbrook**

Special Make-Up Effects Artist
Lance Anderson

Assistant Special Make-Up Effects **Scott Coulter**

Crow Wrangler **Gary Gero**

Animal Trainers **Roger Schumacher**
Larry Madrid

Wardrobe Supervisor **Darryl Levine**

Costumers **Marina Marit Roberta Bile**

Set Costumes **Pauline White Amy Lilley**

Assistant Costumer **Janet Schriever**

Seamstress **C.J. Harris**

Make-Up Artists **Sharon Ilson Herita Jones**

Assistant Make-Up Artists
Sandra Orsolyak Tiger Tate

Key Hairstylists **Michelle Johnson**
Mary Lampert

Assistant Hairstylists **Shelly Hutchins**
Rita Troy

Propmasters **Daniel Kuttner Tantar Leviser**

Assistant Propmaster **Charlene Hamer**

Weapons Specialist **Jim Moyer**

Special Effects **J.B. Jones**

Special Effects Foreman **James Roberts**

Gaffer **Claudio Miranda**

Best Boy Electric **Steve Perry**

Electric **Al Demayo**

Key Grip **Charles "Chunky" Huse**

Best Boy Grips **Robert Hoelen Scott Hillman**

Dolly Grips **Jeffrey Howery Scott Lefridge**

Additional Editors **Sonny Baskin Craig Woods**

1st Assistant Editors **Matthew Booth**
Richard Aldrete

2nd Assistant Editors **John Finklea**
Patrick Mullane

Apprentice Editor **Tony Max**

Supervising Sound Editors **Dave McMoyler**
John J. Miceli

Supervising Sound Designer **Joseph Phillips**

Sound Designer **Brian McPhearson**

Dialogue Editors **Patrick Sellers Jeff Watts**
Glenn T. Morgan Dan Hegeman

Crow Voice Design **David Kneupper**

Sound Effects Editors **Peter Lehman**
Chris Assells Scott Mosteller Amy Hoffberg

Foley Editor **Robert Batha**

Assistant Sound Editors **John Rice**
Ian Marshall Ishmell Curry Rodney Sharp

Additional Sound Recording
Anthony Miceli and Kim Waugh

Music Editor **Richard Bernstein**

Assistant Music Editors **Berlau Picard**
Philip Tallman

Orchestration **Tim Simonec**

Music Sound Design **Brian Williams**

Post Consultation **Michael Harker**

Production Accountants **Sam Bernstein**
Bill Rose, Jr.

Assistant Production Accountants
Grace Griffith Steve Simpson
Jean Henri Ahearn, Sr.
Christopher R. Dotterweich

Payroll Assistant **Gregor Wilson**

Financial Consultant **Curt Schroeder**

Script Supervisor **Cornelia "Nini" Rogan**

Location Manager **Vick Griffin**

Production Coordinators **Jennifer Roth**
Carrie Durose

Production Secretary **Cindy Gray**

Additional Second Assistant Directors
Danielle Rigby Chemen Ochoa
Stephanie Adams Jay Tobias
Cynthia Williams

Production Assistants **Chad Rosen**
Patrick Lawlor Patrick Marz

L.A. Production Assistants **Tad Winship**
Bruce Hofert Emily Zalenski
Michael Toay Nina Dib

Assistant to Mr. Lee **Eliza Hutton**

Assistants to Mr. Pressman
Michael Radiloff Christopher Otto

Assistant to Mr. Proyas **Janice Biggs**

Assistant to Mr. Most **Stacy Plavoukos**

Assistant to Ms. Cherry **Leslie Reed**

Business Affairs Executive **Daniel Posener**

Transportation Coordinator **Lee Siler**

Transportation Captain **Jesse Smith**

Casting Associates **Kerry Barden**
Diana Jaher Jennifer Low Sauer

Extras Casting **Craig and Lisa Fincannon**

Extras Casting Associate **Pam Plummer**

Voice Casting **Barbara Harris**

Unit Publicist
Jason D. Scott – Clein + White, Inc.

Craft Service **Reva Grantham**

Brandon Lee's Trainer **Darryl Chan**

Teacher **Ruth Streszoff**

Medics **Clyde Baisey Dione Kirby**

Caterers **Art Hoover and Ken Young**

Miniature Photography Photographed at
Dream Quest Images

Producer of Miniature Photography
Robert Stadd

Director of Photography (Miniatures)
Michael Talarico

Motion Control Programmers
Terry Moews

Mac Motion Control Gaffer
Scott Campbell

Motion Control Technicians
Richard Johnson and George Prior

Model Coordinator **Gus Ramsden**

Chief Model Maker **Eric Skipper**

Model Makers **Richard Wright**
Eric Skipper, Jr. James McGeachy
Jinnie Eddlemon

Dream Quest Editor **Deborah Wolff**

Dream Quest Assistant Editor
Shawn Broes

Coordinator **Warren Farina**

Digital Compositing by
Motion Pixel Corporation
A Division of Dream Quest Images

DIGITAL COMPOSITING CREW

Executive Producer **Mark M. Galvin**

Producer **David K. McCullough**

Production Manager **Melissa Cira Taylor**

Technical Supervisors **Howard Burdick**
Tim Landry

Digital Matte Artists **Karen deJong**
Bob Scifo

Compositing Technicians **Heather Davis**
Blaine Kennison Ron Longo
John T. Murrah Mary Nelson
Alexandra A. Pitt

Digital Roto Artists **Oliver Sarda**

Scanning/Output Technician
Jason Piccioni

Visual Effects Editor **Derrick Mitchell**

Visual Effects Assistant Editor
Kim Jorgensen

Post Production Sound Services
Provided By
Skywalker Sound
A Division of Lucas Digital, Ltd.
Santa Monica, California

Re-recording Mixers **Matthew Jadarola**
Gary Gegan Gover Helsley

Additional Re-Recording Mixers
Thomas P. Gerard Christian Minkler
Ken Polk

Stage Recordist **Robin Johnston**

Stage Loader **Bryan Fowler**

ADR & Foley Stages
J.B. & Associates, Inc.
Todd-AO Studios East

ADR Mixers **Marilyn Graf**
Paul Zydel

Foley Mixer **Eric Hoeschen**

ADR & Foley Recordist **Brian Smith**

Foley Artists **Joe Sabella Doug Reed**

Dolby Stereo Consultant **Dan Sperry**

Negative Cutter **Gary Burritt**

Color Timer **Steve Sheridan**

Optical Negative **N.T. Audio Visual**
Thomas McCormick

Video Transfers **RTV Video**

Sound Transfers **Acme Soundworks**

Optical Effects
International Creative Effects
Burbank, CA

Color By **Deluxe**

Studio Facilities **Carolco Studios, Inc.**

Camera & Lens Equipment
Joe Dunton & Company

Crowvision Lense By **Joe Dunton**

Burn
Written by Robert Smith, Simon Gallup,
Boris Williams, and Perry Bamonte
Performed by The Cure
Courtesy of Fiction Records Ltd. and Elektra Entertainment

Golgotha Tenement Blues
Written by Scott Benzel, Mike Fisher, and Stuart Kupers
Performed by Machines of Loving Grace
Courtesy of Mammoth Records

Big Empty
Written by Dean DeLeo and Scott Weiland
Performed by Stone Temple Pilots
Courtesy of Atlantic Recording Corporation

Color Me Once
Written by Gordon Gano and Brian Ritchie
Performed by Violent Femmes
Courtesy of Slash Records

Dead Souls
Written by Ian Curtis, Peter Hook,
Bernard Sumner, and Stephen Morris
Performed by Nine Inch Nails
Courtesy of Nothing /TVT Interscope Records

Darkness
Written by Rage Against the Machine
Performed by Rage Against the Machine
Courtesy of Epic Associated

Ghostrider
Written by Martin Rev and Alan Vega
Performed by Rollins Band
Courtesy of Imago Recording Company

Snakedriver
Written by William Reid and Jim Reid
Performed by Jesus and the Mary Chain
Courtesy of Blanco Y Negro/American Recordings

Time Baby II
Written by Jim Goodall, Brad Laner, Jim Putnam,
Ed Ruscha, and Beth Thompson
Performed by Medicine
Courtesy of American Recordings

After The Flesh
Written by Buzz McCoy and Groovie Mann
Performed by My Life with the Thrill Kill Kult
Courtesy of Interscope Records

Milktoast
Written by Page Nye Hamilton
Performed by Helmet
Courtesy of Interscope Records

The Badge
Written by Tom Roberts and Jerry Lang
Performed by Pantera
Courtesy of EastWest Records America

Slip Slide Melting
Written by For Love Not Lisa
Performed by For Love Not Lisa
Courtesy of East West Records America

It Can't Rain All The Time
Written by Graeme Revell and Jane Siberry
Performed by Jane Siberry
Courtesy of Reprise Records

Special Thanks to
Lynn Pressman Raymond

Production/Financing Counsel
Pryor, Cashman, Sherman & Flynn
James A. Janowitz Karen Robson
Phyllis Kaufman Roger Kass

Insurance **Great Northern Brokerage**

Completion Guarantor **Film Finances, Inc.**

This motion picture was filmed entirely
in Wilmington, North Carolina and
Los Angeles, California.

The Digital Experience
DTA in Selected Theatres
Dolby Stereo in Selected Theatres

Certificate Number #32859

From Atlantic #82519 THE CROW soundtrack available on compact discs and cassettes.

If the people we love

are stolen from us,

the way to have them live on

is to never stop loving them.

Buildings burn, people die,

but real love is forever.